Heinemann EXPLORE Science

Student Book

New International Edition

Grade 3

Tara Lievesley, Deborah Herridge
Series editor: John Stringer

WAYS LEARNING

PEARSON

Pearson Education Limited is a company incorporated in England and Wales having its registered office at Edinburgh Gate, Harlow, Essex, CM20 2JE.

Registered company number: 872828

www.pearsonglobalschools.com

Text © Pearson Education Limited 2012
First published 2003. This edition published 2012.

16 15 14 13 12
IMP 10 9 8 7 6 5 4 3 2 1

British Library Cataloguing in Publication Data
A catalogue record for this book is available from the British Library

ISBN 978 0 435 13357 3

Edited by Pat Winfield
Designed by Scout Design Associates
Original illustrations © Pearson Education Limited, 2003, 2009, 2012
Illustrated by Simon Rumble, Beehive Illustration Ltd and TechSet Ltd
Picture research by Louise Edgeworth
Cover photo/illustration © Alamy Images
Indexed by Indexing Specialists (UK) Ltd
Printed and bound in Malaysia, CTP-KHL

Acknowledgements
The publisher would like to thank the following for their kind permission to reproduce their photographs:

(Key: b-bottom; c-centre; l-left; r-right; t-top)

Alamy Images: Steve Hamblin. Alamy 59; **Brand X Pictures**: Morey Milbradt 34b; **Corbis**: Corbis 66, Fancy. Veer 34t, Jim Sugar 67; **Digital Stock**: Digital Stock 14b; **Fotolia.com**: Africa Studio 29, blas 61, Frog 974 55bl, gozzoli 60b, Max Tactic 65, nutsiam 3, Pavel Losevsky 4, pavelr 57, Rich Lindie 2b, Rido 10b, Rob 1, Shalom 25br, Tomo Jesenicnik 25tr, vgm6 14t, Vladitto 46l, wiedzma 21t, Yuriy Poznukhov 25bl, Юрий Чесноков 25tl; **Getty Images**: 41cl; **Imagestate Media**: Imagestate. John Foxx Collection 60c; **National Geophysical Data Center**: National Geophysical Data Center. G.E. Ulrich. Hawaii Volcano Observatory. U.S. Geological Survey 53; **Pearson Education Ltd**: Trevor Clifford 40tr, 70, Coleman Yuen 27, Debbie Rowe 36cr, Malcolm Harris 31, 33t, 36b, Rob Judges 42, 74r, Rob Judges 42, 74r, Tudor Photography 43, 68t; **PhotoDisc**: Photolink 88bl, Photolink / F. Schussler 38, Photolink / S. Meltzer 71; **Photolibrary.com**: Lushpix. Unlisted Images. photolibrary.com 52; Science Photo Library Ltd: CHARLES D. WINTERS 54, RICHARD MEGNA / FUNDAMENTAL 80, THOMAS WIEWANDT / VISUALS UNLIMITED, INC. 55t; **Shutterstock.com**: 12tr, 28tr, 37tr, Andy Dean Photography 8b, Anette Linnea Rasmussen 90, Anna segeren 88br, Baloncici 33b, Dennis Michael Photography 23, Dmitry Rukhlenko 39, Dwight Smith 55br, EPG_EuroPhotoGraphics 24, forestpath 18, Fotokostic 6b, G2019 45t, Gergo Orban 10t, GraÃ§a Victoria 49r, greenphile 49l, Jessmine 74l, Karel Gallas 60t, Martin M303 28c, michael sheehan 14c, Mogens Trolle 6tl, monbibi 73, Nordling 82b, Olga Popova 82t, Palmer Kane LLC 5, Pangfolio.com 68b, Paul Morris 69, Photobac 2t, photokup 21b, Rafa Irusta 8t, Rob Byron 19, Robert Hoetink 88t, Rohit Seth 7, RTimages 6tr, Serg Zastavkin 45c, szefei 32, Thomas M Perkins 9, tlorna 46r, Vacclav 45b

All other images © Pearson Education

Every effort has been made to trace the copyright holders and we apologise in advance for any unintentional omissions. We would be pleased to insert the appropriate acknowledgement in any subsequent edition of this publication.

Contents

How to use this book

At the beginning of each Unit there are lists of things you should already know or be able to do.

This shows words in the Unit that are important. Learn and use them.

This box tells you what the lesson is about.

Find out what coloured words in bold mean in the Glossary at the back of the book.

Think about these questions. By the end of the Unit you will know how to answer them.

Try these activities. Your teacher will help you.

These boxes give you some fascinating facts.

Unit 1: Living and growing

Humans and animals need to eat to live and grow. As we grow from child to adult, we need to eat a good balanced diet. This will include foods from all the different food groups in the right amounts. Our teeth are vital to eating and we need to care for them so they last well. Different types of teeth are good for different types of food. Crocodiles and sheep eat different things so their teeth are different.

What do you know?

- You need to eat to grow and be healthy.
- You should eat a variety of foods.
- Foods are divided into different groups.
- You should eat a balanced diet to be healthy.
- All animals need to eat food to be healthy and active, but not all foods are good for all animals.
- We need to plan a diet carefully.
- We usually use our teeth to eat.

Words to learn

bacteria, canine, carbohydrate, carnivore, cavity, crown, decay, diet, energy, fats, hearing, herbivore, incisor, mineral, molar, nutrition, omnivore, plaque, premolar, protein, receptors, reproduce, result, senses, sight, smell, taste, touch, vitamin

Skills check

Can you...
- decide what evidence and measurements to take?
- say if your evidence and results are strong?

Let's find out...

Your teeth are special! When you visit the dentist, she looks at your teeth to see if they are healthy. Why does she want you to clean your teeth after every meal? Why might she ask you to floss between your teeth? What else can you do to keep your teeth healthy?

Unit 1: Living and growing 1

Food types

Things to learn

- All animals, including humans, need food and water to stay alive, grow and be active.
- The process of eating food and how our bodies use food and drink is called nutrition.
- All foods can be placed in groups. We need to eat food from each group to stay healthy.

Growing up

We all need to eat and drink to live and grow. We don't all eat the same things, or the same amount.

We couldn't eat as much food as an elephant!

This baby needs to eat a lot to grow as big as its mother.

Where do you get your energy?

If you play sports, you have to eat properly. You need foods that provide energy. Some foods provide more energy than others. Think of some examples.

What should you eat?

There are four main groups of food. You should eat something from each group every day. Some foods give us energy to do sport.

Carbohydrates, such as rice or bread, give us rapid energy.

Proteins, such as meat, fish pulses and nuts help us grow.

Fats, such as butter and oil, give us a store of energy and help keep us warm.

Vitamins and minerals from fruits and vegetables help keep us healthy.

This meal has something from every food group.

I wonder...

If I ate a cheeseburger, fries and an apple pie for lunch, would any food group be missing?

Things to do

Putting food into groups
- Draw a picture of all the foods you ate yesterday. Place a label on each food to show which group it belongs to. Which food groups did you miss?
- Plan a balanced meal for tonight. Don't forget your drinks!

Dig deeper

Find out:
- which foods are good for helping you to grow strong.

Did you know?

- In the past, many people died from not eating enough vitamin C. There is vitamin C in fresh fruit and vegetables.
- During your lifetime you will eat about 27 tonnes of food. That's about the weight of six elephants.
- It takes more energy to eat and digest a piece of celery than the energy it contains.

6 Heinemann Explore Science Grade 3

Unit 1: Living and growing 7

This box tells you what you will find out during the lesson. Your teacher will help you.

Clean teeth

Your challenge
● Find out the best way to clean your teeth.
● Decide how to collect the evidence.
● Is the evidence detailed enough?

Which way is best for cleaning your teeth?

My granny just rinses her teeth with water.

My mum says toothpaste helps to kill the bacteria in our mouths.

My brother just brushes his teeth without toothpaste.

We could use a light sensor to see how clean the sheet is.

We could photograph our sheets after each experiment.

We could hold the sheet up to the light to see how clean it is.

What you need
● toothpaste
● toothbrushes
● plastic sheets
● a permanent marker

What to do
Class 3 students want to find the best way to clean their teeth. They are going to use clear plastic with marker-pen **stains** on and clean it using different methods.

Which of their ideas would you choose?

What to check
Now try it yourselves.
● What are you going to measure?
● How will you collect your evidence?
● How will you make it a **fair test**?
● Which way of cleaning do you think will be best?

What did you find?

One group in Class 3 used the light sensor to record how clean the sheet was. Here are their results.

Method of cleaning	Light sensor reading
Toothpaste only	2
Toothpaste and brushing	27
Toothpaste and lots of brushing	35
Brushing only	15
Rinse in water only	0

● Draw a chart of your results or Class 3's results. Use a computer program to record your results, then draw a chart.
● Think about what your chart shows. Which method of cleaning was best? How can you tell? Why do you think that was?

Can you do better?
How good is your evidence?
What would you do differently if you tried this again?

Now predict
Class 3 students have been given some different-shaped toothbrushes to test. What advice could you give them about carrying out a fair test investigation?

Yassmin and Aisha use different toothpastes. They are trying to guess which is best for cleaning teeth. How could you **predict** which one would be best? Why?

Use what you have learned to answer these questions.

Unit 1: Review

What have you learned?
● You know that all animals eat, move, grow and reproduce.
● You know that humans have five senses.
● You know that exercise is important for a healthy lifestyle.
● You know that all animals need water and a good, varied diet to grow and be active and healthy.
● You can name some foods that provide energy and some that help us grow.
● You can name the four types of human teeth and what they do.
● You know that not all animals eat the same foods.
● You know why we must look after our teeth.
● You can record information in drawings, tables and charts.

Find out more about...
● how we can keep healthy
● how Louis Pasteur **preserved** food.

Check-up
Esher is writing a report about health and fitness. He has talked to a nurse and a dentist about how to stay fit and healthy. What could he write as:
● a healthy diet sheet for a day's food?
● the instructions for using toothpaste?

The answer!
Do you remember the question about why you visit the dentist? Cleaning your teeth removes the plaque that builds up. Plaque is caused by the bacteria that grow on your teeth. Some bacteria live in the gaps between your teeth. Your toothbrush can't always reach them, but flossing will! A mouthwash will help kill any bacteria still left after brushing.

Here you find answers to important questions.

Check what you have learned.

Unit 1: Living and growing

Humans and animals need to eat to live and grow. As we grow from child to adult, we need to eat a good balanced **diet**. This will include foods from all the different food groups in the right amounts. Our teeth are vital to eating and we need to care for them so they last well. Different types of teeth are good for different types of food. Crocodiles and sheep eat different things so their teeth are different.

What do you know?

- You need to eat to grow and be healthy.
- You should eat a variety of foods.
- Foods are divided into different groups.
- You should eat a balanced diet to be healthy.
- All animals need to eat food to be healthy and active, but not all foods are good for all animals.
- We need to plan a diet carefully.
- We usually use our teeth to eat.

Skills check

Can you...

- decide what evidence and measurements to take?
- say if your evidence and **results** are strong?

Let's find out...

Your teeth are special! When you visit the dentist, she looks at your teeth to see if they are healthy. Why does she want you to clean your teeth after every meal? Why might she ask you to **floss** between your teeth? What else can you do to keep your teeth healthy?

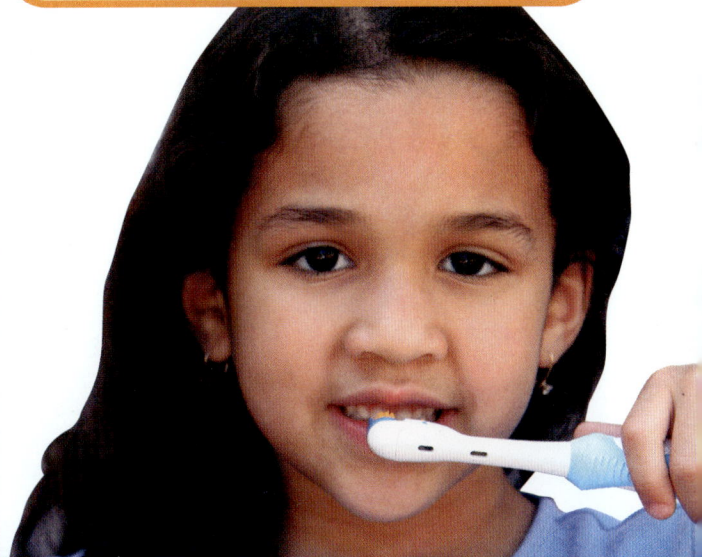

Words to learn

bacteria
canine
carbohydrate
carnivore
cavity
crown
decay
diet
energy
fats

hearing
herbivore
incisor
mineral
molar
nutrition
omnivore
plaque
premolar
protein

receptors
reproduce
result
senses
sight
smell
taste
touch
vitamin

I'm special

Things to learn

● All animals eat, move, grow and **reproduce**.

New you

You are unique. There never was, and never will be, anybody exactly like you. You are like both your parents, but you are very special. You are growing and changing and, like animals, you can eat and move. One day, you may be a parent. Your children will be unique too.

A young penguin chick being fed by its parent

Animals need food and water

Unlike plants, animals cannot make their own food. Animals need to eat and drink. Animals need to move around to find or catch the food they need. Young animals are fed by their parents until they can find food for themselves.

Growing and changing

Animals get bigger, but they don't **swell** up like a balloon. As they eat and drink, they add to themselves. As they grow, animals can do more and more. You are growing and changing. What could you do when you were a baby? What can you do now? How have you changed since you were a baby? How will you change in the future?

Things to do

How are you growing and changing?

- Find a picture of you as a baby. Find a recent picture of you. Look at both of them. How are you different? How have you changed? Find out how much you weighed when you were a baby. How much do you weigh now?
- Look at your baby picture again. How many teeth did you have then? How many teeth have you got today? How many new teeth have grown?

Dig deeper

Find out:
- more about animal young
- how young mammals are fed differently from other animals.

I wonder...

Why are some twins identical – but some are not?

Did you know?

- Humans are animals too!
- Some children are twins. They may be identical. That means they look the same. But even they are unique.
- You are mostly water. Three-quarters of your body is water and without it you are just a big bag of chemicals!
- The tiny Jerboa **rodent** never drinks! It gets all the water it needs from its food.

Things to learn

- Humans have five senses.
- We use our senses to learn about our world.

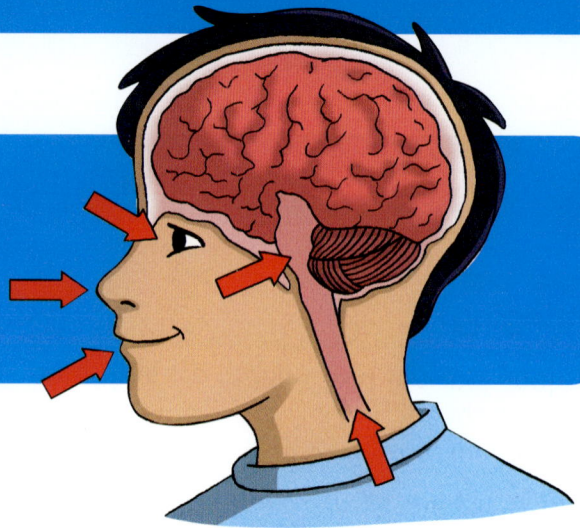

Here are the five senses. Touch is shown by the arrow at the bottom.

Five fabulous senses

We have five fabulous senses that help us learn about our world. They are:

- hearing, to hear music, people talking and many other sounds
- sight, to see colours, shapes and movement
- touch, to feel soft, hard, hot and cold things all around us
- smell, to enjoy the **scents** of home cooking and bonfires
- taste, to taste our favourite foods.

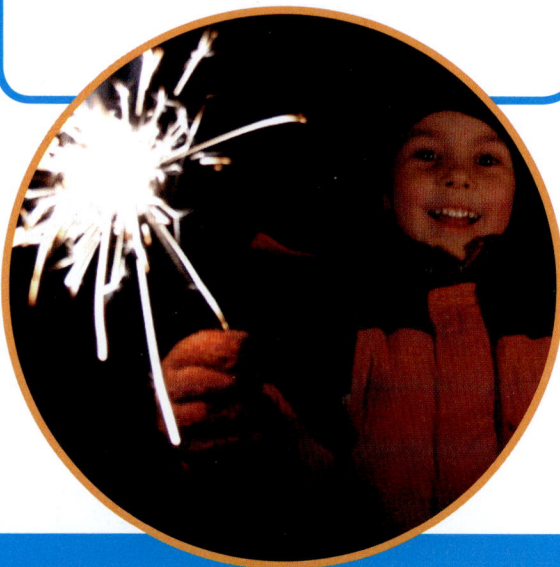

Very receptive

The parts of our body that sense things are called the sense organs. There are special parts of each sense organ called receptors. These receptors send information to your brain along long nerve cells. That way your brain knows what's happening around you. The receptors in different parts of your body respond to different things. You can't taste through your ears or hear through your eyes!

Sight and hearing

Some people are born blind (unable to see) or deaf (unable to hear). Others become blind or deaf through accidents or illness. People wear glasses or hearing aids to improve their sight or hearing. Imagine if you lost one of your senses. How would your world change?

Things to do

Using your senses

Make a sensory map of your school. Stop on your journey around school. Record what you hear on a digital recorder. Draw a picture of some of the shapes you see around you. Make rubbings with paper and **wax** crayons of textures that you can feel or take photographs. Make a 'scent poem' to describe the different smells in different places.

Why have we left out 'taste'? Why is it not safe to taste things around school?

Dig deeper

Find out:
- about sign language
- about Louis Braille. He developed a code of raised dots so blind people could use their sense of touch to read.

I wonder…

We say 'as blind as a bat', but are bats really blind?

Did you know?

- Some dogs can smell much better than we can. Police use specially trained dogs to hunt for drugs and explosives by scent.
- A grasshopper hears through an organ on its knees!
- Babies' eyes aren't fully grown when they are born. They can't see well for a few months.

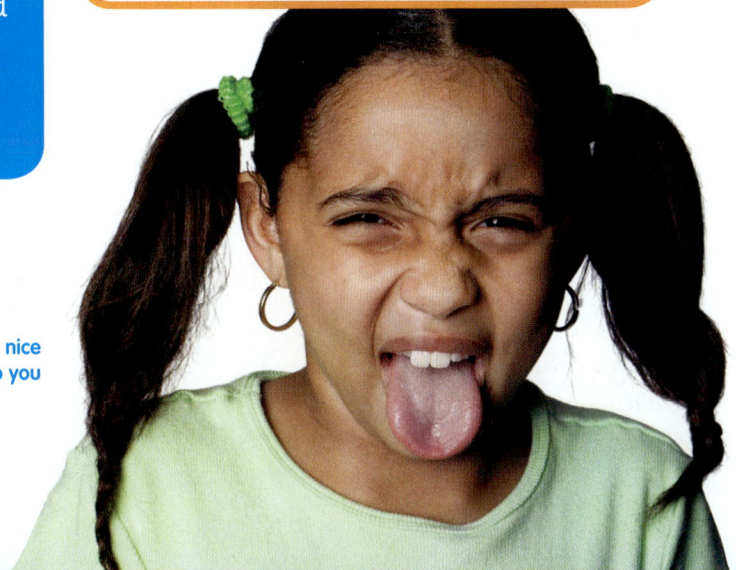

Foods can taste nice or nasty to you

Food types

Things to learn

- All animals, including humans, need food and water to stay alive, grow and be active.
- The process of eating food and how our bodies use food and drink is called **nutrition**.
- All foods can be placed in groups. We need to eat food from each group to stay healthy.

Growing up

We all need to eat and drink to live and grow. We don't all eat the same things, or the same amount.

We couldn't eat as much food as an elephant!

This baby needs to eat a lot to grow as big as its mother

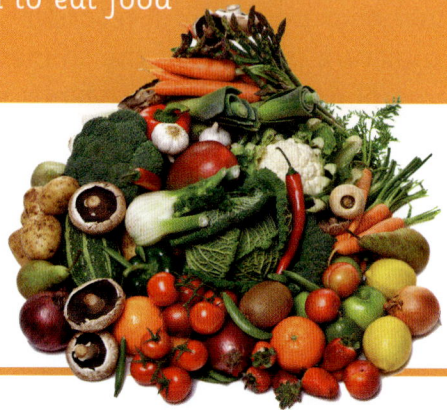

What should you eat?

There are four main groups of food. You should eat something from each group every day. Some foods give us energy to do sport.

Carbohydrates, such as rice or bread, give us rapid energy.

Proteins, such as meat, fish pulses and nuts help us grow.

Fats, such as butter and oil, give us a store of energy and help keep us warm.

Vitamins and **minerals** from fruits and **vegetables** help keep us healthy.

Where do you get your energy?

If you play sports, you have to eat properly. You need foods that provide **energy**. Some foods provide more energy than others. Think of some examples.

This meal has something from every food group

I wonder...

If I ate a cheeseburger, fries and an apple pie for lunch, would any food group be missing?

Things to do

Putting food into groups

- Draw a picture of all the foods you ate yesterday. Place a label on each food to show which group it belongs to. Which food groups did you miss?
- Plan a balanced meal for tonight. Don't forget your drinks!

Dig deeper

Find out:
- which foods are good for helping you to grow strong.

Did you know?

- In the past, many people died from not eating enough vitamin C. There is vitamin C in fresh fruit and vegetables.
- During your lifetime you will eat about 27 tonnes of food. That's about the weight of six elephants.
- It takes more energy to eat and **digest** a piece of celery than the energy it contains.

Healthy eating

Things to learn

- You need to eat a variety of foods to stay healthy.
- A diet is not only for losing weight.
- You must prepare and store food carefully to stay healthy.

The same, but different

Make sure you have enough to eat of the right sorts of food. Some people eat different diets.

A vegetarian doesn't eat any meat, but eats other foods such as lentils and beans. These provide the protein (growth food) they are not getting from meat. This means they are still healthy.

Different cultures eat different diets. What diet does your family eat?

An apple a day...

People in Britain and America say, 'An apple a day keeps the doctor away'. An apple is a fruit, which means it gives us vitamins and minerals. Our body needs these to keep healthy. Can you explain why this saying might be true?

Too much and too little

If you eat too much of the wrong foods, you may become overweight. What sorts of food would make you overweight? How are they alike?

You can also become unhealthy if you don't eat enough. What would happen to you if you didn't eat enough?

Healthy diets

- Vegetarians don't eat any meat or fish. They still need food for energy, growth, warmth and health.
- Plan a healthy diet for a vegetarian.
- Make sure you include something from each food group. Avoid too many sweet or fatty foods.

Dig deeper

Find out:
- which foods we should eat less of
- how to store food to stop it harming us.

I wonder...

Think about a meal of chicken curry, rice and naan bread. Why are plants needed to produce each part of the meal?

Did you know?

- The French Emperor Napoleon asked three scientists to find a way to store food safely. Francois Appert **invented** canned food. But can-openers were not invented until 48 years later!
- Flamingos are pink because of a chemical in the shrimps they eat. This chemical is in carrots too. If we ate nothing but carrots, our skin would start to look orange.

Keeping active

Things to learn

- Exercise is important for a healthy life.
- Exercise keeps us fit.
- Exercise keeps our hearts healthy.

Getting moving

We **exercise** all the time, even without knowing it!

Just walking or running about, dancing, doing household jobs, playing ball games and getting our bodies moving is exercise. When we exercise, we are helping our bodies build strong bones and muscles that we need to be able to move and live. Doing some sort of exercise every day keeps us fit and healthy.

Staying strong

Exercise can make all of your muscles stronger. When you use your muscles to do powerful things such as rowing, swinging on monkey bars or doing push-ups, you build up your strength.

A healthy heart

The heart is a vital muscle that pumps blood around the body. Exercise helps your heart get stronger.

When you run or play sports, you start to breathe harder and faster. This means that you take more oxygen into your body, which helps it work better. Exercise like this is called aerobic exercise. Aerobic means 'with air'. Aerobic exercise can make your heart beat faster. If you exercise like this regularly then your heart becomes stronger.

How many different aerobic activities can you think of?

Keeping active can make you a winner

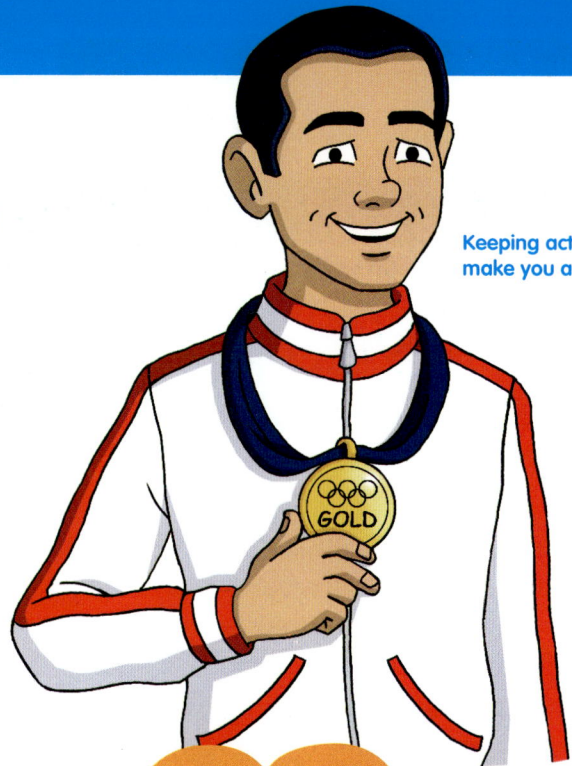

Lifestyle coach

This is Jalal. He spends his days on the sofa in front of the television and never does any exercise. Be his lifestyle coach and give him some advice.

- How can Jalal increase his activity levels in his everyday life?
- Which activities would be good aerobic exercise?
- Which activities would help build strong muscles?
- What else might Jalal do to become healthier?

I wonder...

Is it possible to have too much exercise?

Did you know?

- Some Olympic athletes have **asthma**. They have learned to control it when they exercise.
- Taking the stairs instead of an escalator or lift is a great way to get exercise.

A question of balance

Things to learn

- Eating a balanced diet is important for good health.
- A balanced diet and enough exercise together can keep us healthy.

Too much or not enough?

Being overweight can hurt your body. It's harder to be active if you are overweight. It can make you feel tired and give you painful joints. Eating too much of the wrong sorts of food is bad for us. But if we don't eat enough of the right sorts of food we can become very underweight. This can hurt us too.

Fruits such as these grapes should form part of our daily diet

Just right

The food you eat can keep you healthy or it can make you ill. Making healthy food choices can keep you well. This doesn't mean that you can never eat sweets or fatty foods again. It just means that you need to eat more of the food which is good for you. Eat less of the food that can harm you. You need to try to get the balance just right. Part of being healthy is being a healthy weight. You can do this by balancing the energy you get from food against the energy you use by being active.

Fantastic five

Doctors think that including five portions of fruit and vegetables each day in our diets is good for us.

We should reduce the amounts of sugar and fat that we eat. We should cut down on junk food and ready meals.

What do you think? What could you change about your diet to make it healthier?

Things to do

Balanced choices

Do you remember Jalal? He's taking exercise now and feels better. What else could he do to be healthy?

- Plan a menu for a day in Jalal's life. What should you include? He is allowed small **treats** from time to time.
- Jalal drinks a lot of fizzy, sugary drinks. Can you suggest a healthier drink?

Dig deeper

Find out:
- how much exercise children need every day to stay healthy
- how the nutritional values of food are measured.

I wonder...

Which exercise is best for you?

Did you know?

- The first fruit eaten on the Moon was a peach.
- Carrots were originally purple. Orange varieties were developed 400 years ago.
- Most people walk at about 4.8 kilometres an hour (3 miles an hour). If you walked at this pace and didn't stop, it would take 18 days to walk from Mumbai to Kolkata, across India.

Animal food

Things to learn

- Different animals have different diets.
- Herbivores eat plants and carnivores eat meat.

Domesticated animals

Domesticated animals that we keep at home or on farms began as wild animals. Dogs were once wolves and house cats were much larger cats. Now they eat tinned or dried food. What sorts of food do you think they ate in the wild?

Gerbils and rabbits are herbivores. Gerbils are known as 'desert rats'. In Europe you sometimes see wild rabbits in fields.

Domesticated animals don't search for food anymore. How do we decide what food to give them?

Favourite foods

Giraffes are **herbivores**. They eat the leaves from acacia trees, which are very **thorny**. They reach the juiciest leaves using their long tongues. The tongues curl around the thorns, so they don't get hurt.

Lions don't eat many plants. They eat meat and are **carnivores**. They run fast and have sharp claws and teeth to catch their food.

Animals that eat both plants and other animals are called **omnivores**.

Things to do

Feeding time

Maya works in a zoo and feeds the animals. Sometimes she gets confused about who eats what and how much.

- Decide how to help Maya so that she always knows what to feed each animal.
- What questions might you ask Maya to help her?

I wonder…

Watch the way that a herbivore eats its food. Which teeth does it use most? Which way does its lower jaw move?

Dig deeper

Find out:
- what different animals eat
- which animals eat other animals.

Did you know?

- When mouse-flavoured cat food was tested on cats, they didn't like it!
- Cats may kill something and bring it to their owners as a gift. So if you see a dead animal on the doorstep, it means your cat likes you!
- An elephant eats mainly leaves and bark. It will eat about 250 kg of food every day. That's like eating a car full of food!

Things to learn

- There are different types of teeth in our mouths.
- Each differently shaped tooth has a particular job to do.

How many teeth?

We have four different types of teeth in our mouths. They have different names and jobs.

Incisors are used for cutting and snipping food.

Canines are the 'fangs' or pointed teeth that grip and hold food.

Molars and **premolars** are for **crushing**, **grinding** and chewing our food so we can swallow it easily.

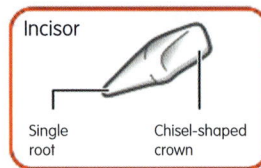

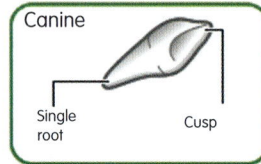

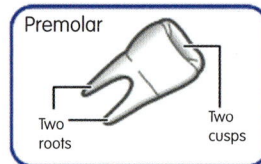

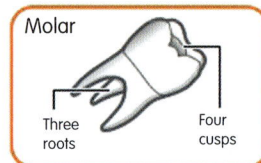

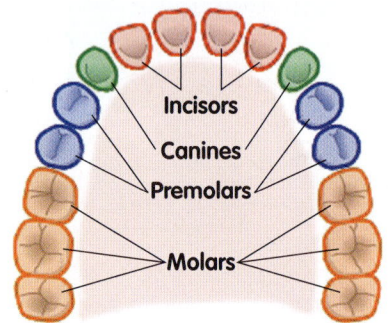

Incisor
Single root — Chisel-shaped crown

Canine
Single root — Cusp

Premolar
Two roots — Two cusps

Molar
Three roots — Four cusps

Incisors
Canines
Premolars
Molars

This picture only shows one half of a human mouth

Incisors
These eight sharp teeth are like knives that slice into food.

Canines
These four long, sharp teeth stab and grip food.

Premolars
Eight premolars have flat tops and two sharp ridges. They tear and grind food.

Molars
These 12 large teeth have flat bumpy tops that grind together to chew food into small pieces.

Teeth are our own cutlery!

Knives were invented long ago. They are like our incisors and cut food. Forks are more recent. Our canines can be used for gripping our food – like forks.

Things to do

Which job?

Look at your teeth in a mirror. They all do different jobs when you eat.

- Describe each tooth you see.
- Bite into a biscuit. Which teeth do you use? Why are our incisors the best shape for biting and our premolars and molars for chewing? Think about the shape of each tooth.

Other animals' teeth

Different animals have different types of teeth.

- Look at pictures of other animals' teeth.
- Guess which teeth belong to which animal.
- Why do dogs have canines?
- Why do sheep have grinding teeth?

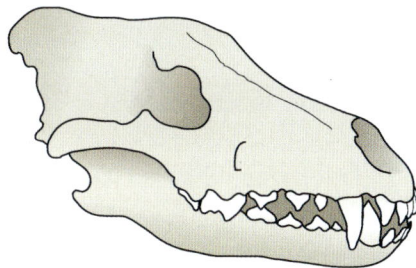

A dog's teeth

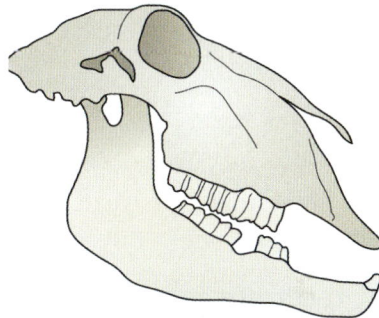

A sheep's teeth

Dig deeper

Find out:
- what your teeth are made of.

I wonder...

If you put a tooth into a glass of cola for a long time, what will happen to it? Can you think why? Why should you brush your teeth after drinking sugary drinks?

Did you know?

- **Vampire bats** have fewer teeth than any other bat because they don't chew their food!
- Rodents' incisors never stop growing. This means they have to gnaw things to grind them down.
- Four hundred years ago, some false teeth were made from wood.

Healthy teeth

Things to learn

● We all have two sets of teeth – milk teeth and adult teeth.
● We must look after our teeth to keep them healthy.
● Some foods can damage our teeth.

Growing teeth

When you were born, you didn't have any teeth. How are you able to swallow your food without **choking**? What sorts of food do babies eat?

Your first teeth are called milk teeth and you have 20 of these. You lose your milk teeth as you grow. Your permanent teeth grow through. You will have 32 of these. Why is it so important to look after them?

How long do we keep them?

Imagine not having any teeth! How would you eat your lunch? If you look after your teeth, you should always have them. But if you don't... you might have to drink your meals! Look at a tooth that has been left in cola. See what sweet foods can do to your teeth...

Dentists use crowns and fillings to mend holes or cavities in some teeth, but if your teeth **decay** and fall out, you will need false ones!

Keeping teeth clean

Your teeth are always covered in living things called bacteria. These **multiply** when you eat something sweet. A white layer called **plaque** builds up. Acid from plaque bacteria **rots** your teeth. It causes cavities.

- You can use a special tablet to colour the plaque red. Place the tablet on your tongue and close your mouth. Rub the tablet over your teeth and gums with your tongue, then look in the mirror.
- The coloured areas are plaque. How can we remove it?

Dig deeper

Find out:
- which foods cause plaque to build up.

I wonder…

Look at a milk tooth and an adult tooth. What differences can you see?

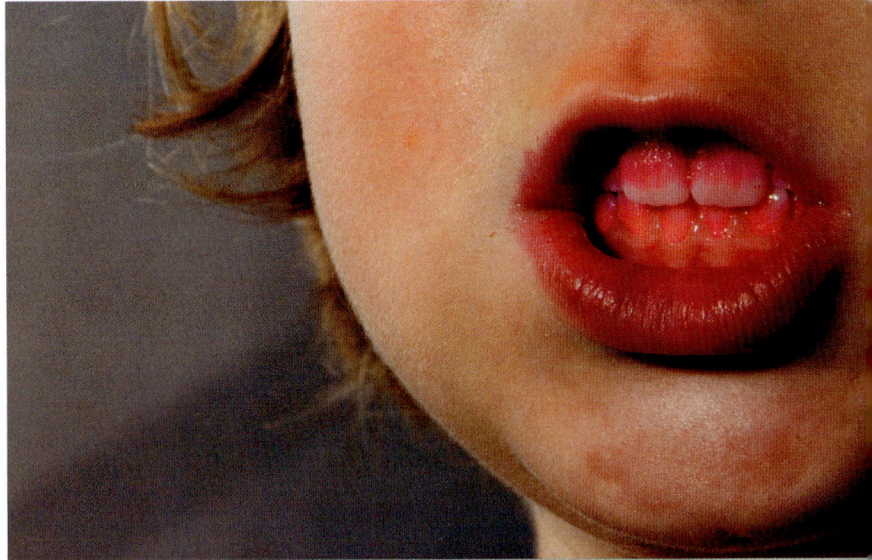

Did you know?

- Even if you ate nothing and only drank pure water, plaque bacteria would still grow on your teeth. When you eat sweets, acid is made in your mouth straight away.
- John Kellogg invented cornflakes for a patient with bad teeth.
- Lions eat leaves and other vegetables to keep their teeth in good condition.

Clean teeth

Your challenge
- Find out the best way to clean your teeth.
- Decide how to collect the evidence.
- Is the evidence detailed enough?

Which way is best for cleaning your teeth?

My granny just rinses her teeth with water.

My mum says toothpaste helps to kill the bacteria in our mouths.

My brother just brushes his teeth without toothpaste.

What you need
- toothpaste
- toothbrushes
- plastic sheets
- a permanent marker

We could use a light sensor to see how clean the sheet is.

We could photograph our sheets after each experiment.

We could hold the sheet up to the light to see how clean it is.

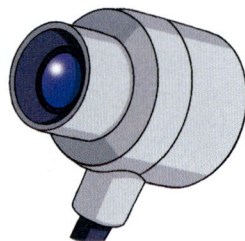

What to do

Class 3 students want to find the best way to clean their teeth. They are going to use clear plastic with marker-pen **stains** on and clean it using different methods.

Which of their ideas would you choose?

What to check

Now try it yourselves.

- What are you going to measure?
- How will you collect your evidence?
- How will you make it a **fair test**?
- Which way of cleaning do you think will be best?

What did you find?

One group in Class 3 used the light sensor to record how clean the sheet was. Here are their results.

Method of cleaning	Light sensor reading
Toothpaste only	2
Toothpaste and brushing	27
Toothpaste and lots of brushing	35
Brushing only	15
Rinse in water only	0

- Draw a chart of your results or Class 3's results. Use a computer program to record your results, then draw a chart.
- Think about what your chart shows. Which method of cleaning was best? How can you tell? Why do you think that was?

Can you do better?

How good is your evidence?

What would you do differently if you tried this again?

Now predict

Class 3 students have been given some different-shaped toothbrushes to test. What advice could you give them about carrying out a fair test investigation?

Yassmin and Aisha use different toothpastes. They are trying to guess which is best for cleaning teeth. How could you **predict** which one would be best? Why?

What have you learned?

- You know that all animals eat, move, grow and reproduce.
- You know that humans have five senses.
- You know that exercise is important for a healthy lifestyle.
- You know that all animals need water and a good, varied diet to grow and be active and healthy.
- You can name some foods that provide energy and some that help us grow.
- You can name the four types of human teeth and what they do.
- You know that not all animals eat the same foods.
- You know why we must look after our teeth.
- You can record information in drawings, tables and charts.

Find out more about...

- how we can keep healthy
- how Louis Pasteur **preserved** food.

Check-up

Esher is writing a report about health and fitness. He has talked to a nurse and a dentist about how to stay fit and healthy. What could he write as:

- a healthy diet sheet for a day's food?
- the instructions for using toothpaste?

The answer!

Do you remember the question about why you visit the dentist? Cleaning your teeth removes the plaque that builds up. Plaque is caused by the bacteria that grow on your teeth. Some bacteria live in the gaps between your teeth. Your toothbrush can't always reach them, but flossing will! A mouthwash will help kill any bacteria still left after brushing.

Unit 2: Helping plants grow well

Plants use the energy of the **Sun** to live and grow. They make the food we eat. Plants produce the gas we breathe – **oxygen**. Healthy, growing plants are essential to you.

What do you know?

- Plants and animals are living things.
- Plants can be sorted into groups.
- Plants need light, water and warmth to grow.
- Growing plants have healthy **leaves**, **stems** and **roots**.
- Plants make their own food. Leaves are the plant's food factories.
- Flowering plants use **seeds** to reproduce.
- Without plants, there would be no people.

Words to learn

energy	pollen
flower	root
germination	seed
leaf	spindly
light	stem
oxygen	thin
pale	warmth
plant	water

Skills check

Can you...

- look closely and make careful observations and measurements?
- collect evidence and decide how good it is?
- use your evidence to explain what you found out?

Let's find out...

You already know that there are different kinds of plants. They have leaves, stems, roots and **flowers**. They need light and water to grow.

Gardeners mainly buy plants at the start of the growing season. Shops make sure that there are young plants for people to buy, but how can they control the way the plants grow, so that they are not too big or too small?

Sorting plants into groups

Things to learn

- Plants and animals are living things.
- Plants can be put in groups using their similarities and differences.
- A branching key asks questions that sort plants into groups.
- These groups of plants have names.

Living and non-living

Living things grow, change and reproduce. They need food and water, and produce waste products. Animals need plants or other animals to eat, but plants produce their own food. Some living things are alike, but others are not. You can use these similarities and differences to group living things.

Different plants

Imagine you had a bunch of flowers of different kinds. You could sort them in many different ways – by colour, by size or by shape. Ask the question 'Has it got one flower on each stem?'. The answer might be 'yes' or 'no'. Put the plants with a single flower in one group. Then another question will separate the plants in this group.

Some plants have flowers

There are many kinds of plants. Some have flowers, some do not. Ferns are plants, but they have no flowers. Some flowers are hard to see. Grass is a plant with green flowers and long, thin leaves. Most trees have broad, flat leaves. Fir trees have green needles instead.

Things to do

Sorting into groups

You need some different plants and two hoops. Sort the plants into the hoops. You might put all the plants with long, thin leaves in one group. The plants with broad leaves go in the other group. Can you group them a different way? Can you explain the reasons for your choices? Now do the same with some flowers – or some pictures of flowers.

Make a branching key

You need pictures of four plants. Ask yourself a question that makes two groups of two. The answer must be 'yes' or 'no'. Now look for a difference between the plants in each group of two. Does it sort them? You have made a branching key.

Dig deeper

Find out:
- more about different types of plants.

I wonder…

Are fungi – such as mushrooms – plants? They have no green colour.

Did you know?

- We group plants and animals in a special way. Carl von Linné invented the system 300 years ago.

Growing plants

Your challenge

- Discover how fast plants can grow.
- Plan a fair test.
- Measure and record the growth of plants.
- Communicate your results.

> I think plants are boring. They never do anything.

> My grandad says they are growing all the time.

> I asked how he knows. Can we test if he is right?

What to do

Decide how you will measure and record your plant's growth. Look at what the children in Class 3 did. You could do everything that they did.

> We will count the leaves every Friday and record the number.

> We will draw our plant every Wednesday.

> We will take a photograph with the digital camera every Monday and Friday.

> We will measure the height of our plant every Monday and record it.

What you need

- small pot plants
- small container to measure water
- a digital camera or a video camera with a timer
- a measuring stick or tape
- a balance or scales

What to check

Now try it yourselves.

- What distance are you going to measure?
- Is this fair?
- What do you think will happen?

What did you find?

One group in Class 3 drew a table of their results. It looked like this.

Week	Height of plant (cm)
start	15
one	17
two	20
three	25
four	31

- Use a computer program to record your results. Draw a chart of your results or Class 3's results. What sort of chart would be best? Look at the charts in your class. Match them to the right plant.
- What does your chart tell you? In your class, which plant grew least? Which plant grew most? Why? Was this what you expected?
- Use your plants, photographs and charts to make a presentation to another class, telling them what you found out.

Large plants can grow from tiny seeds

Can you do better?

Was measuring better than counting?

How could you take different measurements? What would you do differently if you tried this again?

Now predict

Kavita and Jasmin want to buy some plants to grow for the school fair later in the year. They are going to a garden centre. What advice can you give them? How can they choose plants that will grow well?

Roots and stems

Things to learn

- Plants need roots to stay upright.
- Plants need roots to take in water and **nutrients**.
- Plants carry water up the stem to the leaves.

Plants need roots

The larger the plant, the bigger its roots have to be. The underground roots of a tree can be as big as the tree above the ground. The roots help to keep the plant upright and stay firmly in the ground. This helps stop it blowing down.

The roots don't just hold the plant up. They also take in water from the **soil**. Water travels through the stem to every part of the plant.

The water goes up

Why do people put plants in bigger pots as they grow? Bigger plants need more water. To get that water, the plants need bigger roots. Bigger roots need bigger pots. If you move a pot plant from its pot to soil in the garden, it will grow even bigger. Why is that?

Plants need water

You can see the ends of the tubes in a cut celery stem

I wonder...

Hold a leaf up to the light and look through it. How does water get to every part of the leaf?

Things to do

Coloured celery

Celery is the **crunchy** green and white stem of a plant with a lot of small flowers.

- Stand a cut celery stem in water. The water rises up the stem.
- Colour the water with ink or food colouring. Wait a few minutes. What do you see if you carefully cut across the stem?
- Split the base of the stem and put half in one colour and half in another. What happens now? Why?

Dig deeper

Find out:
- why plants need water.

Did you know?

- Thousands of litres of water rush up the trunk of a big tree on hot days.
- Some plants have such long roots to collect water that they stay green even when the grass around them goes brown in hot weather.

Plants and water

Your challenge
- Find out how much water plants and growing seeds need to be healthy.
- Decide how you will collect the evidence.
- Measure and record the growth of plants from seeds.
- Communicate your results.

What to do

Class 3 decided to give seeds different amounts of water to see how they would **germinate** and grow. They then had to decide how to collect the evidence. They decided to use ten seeds for each test.

I've given my plant lots of water.

Don't give it too much.

Why not? I don't want it to dry out.

Plants need some water. We can see how much they need.

I think my plant might need some cola instead.

We will not give our seeds any water.

We will give our seeds a measure of water every day.

The more water the better! We will give our seeds lots of water.

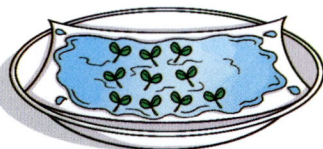

What you need
- small seeds
- saucers and cotton wool
- measuring sticks
- a measuring jug or cylinder
- a digital camera or a video camera with a timer.

What to check
- What do you think will happen?
- What information are you going to collect?

What did you find?

Class 3 drew a table of their results. It looked like this.

Volume of water (cm³)	Number of seeds that germinated after 10 days
0	0
5	10
10	8
15	5
20	2

- Draw a chart of your results or Class 3's results. Use a computer program to record your results. Use it to draw a chart. What kind of chart or graph do you think would be best?
- What does your chart show? How much water was best for the seeds?
- Use your photographs and charts in a PowerPoint presentation to share what you have found out.

A sunflower starting to form a flower bud

Can you do better?

What would you do differently if you tried this again? Would you use the same seeds? Why?

Now predict

- If you want to grow the tallest sunflower, how much water should you give the seeds to help them to germinate? Why water them once they have germinated?
- Why was it a better test to use ten seeds rather than just one?

Plants and light

Things to learn

- Plants need light to grow well.
- Plants use their leaves and light to make food.

Reach for it!

Sunflowers grow very tall. Sometimes they are taller than two people standing on each other's shoulders!

What makes these flowers grow so tall?

Plants need sunlight to make their food. They trap the Sun's energy in their leaves. The food they make is called sugar, which they store as **starch.** Starch provides us with food. When we eat plants, we use the energy of the Sun!

Tall trees

Tall trees in a forest shade smaller trees or plants. This steals the light from the smaller trees, so the tall trees will grow better.

Spreading leaves

If you look up from under a tree, you will see how the leaves spread. The pattern of the leaves helps them catch the most sunlight.

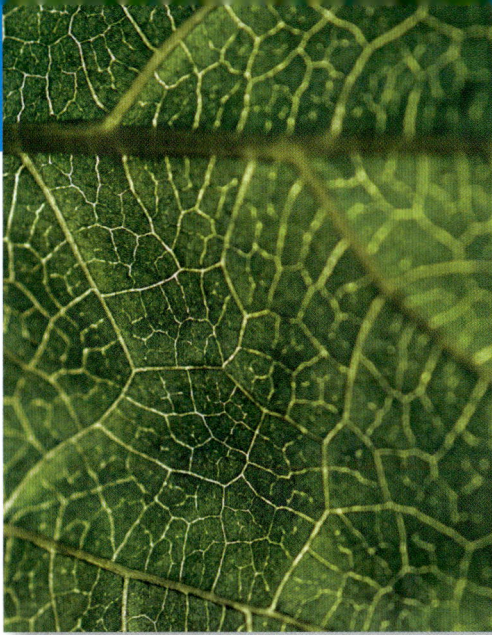
Veins in a magnified leaf

I wonder...

Will a seed begin to grow without light? What would a plant look like if we grew it in a dark cupboard?

Things to do

Why are leaves green?

Plants need light.

- Look at some grass that has grown in the dark. How is it different from grass grown in the light?
- Cut out a foil shape and attach it to the leaf of a plant with a paper clip. Place the plant in a sunny spot and leave it for a week. Take off the foil and look at the leaf. Explain what has happened and why.

Dig deeper

Find out:
- why leaves are green.

Did you know?

- The leaves of the South American Victoria water lily are sometimes over 2 m in diameter.
- Piling soil around celery plants makes the stems grow long and white and good to eat.
- Rhubarb is grown under a bucket with a tiny hole in the top. This forces the rhubarb to grow taller towards the light. The stems, which we eat, grow long.

Rhubarb stems

Plants and warmth

Things to learn

- Plants need warmth to grow well.
- Plants lose water through their leaves.
- Plants grow best when they have warmth, light, air and water.

Warmer and warmer

Plants need warmth to grow big and strong. Gardeners use glasshouses to make their plants grow faster. A glasshouse traps the Sun's heat inside it, which makes it warmer inside the glasshouse than outside. A gardener will start plants growing in a glasshouse, so they are bigger earlier in the year than if they were left outside. This means they may grow to a bigger size, too.

Which vegetable started growing in the glasshouse?

Where does the water go?

When plants get hot or are in the Sun for a long time, they lose water through their leaves. Big, flat leaves lose water easily. Desert plants don't have big, flat leaves.

Things to do

Quick growers

Think back to what you have learned about plants so far.

- How would you grow the biggest and healthiest plants for sandwiches? Where is the best place to start the seeds growing? How much water will you give your young plants? Will you give them light? Why?
- It is a better test to grow more than one seed in any place. Put your seeds on paper towels in dishes and carefully measure how much water you give them. Then put each dish in a different place. What will happen to seeds put in the fridge?

I wonder...

What would happen to life on Earth if the Sun stopped shining?

Dig deeper

Find out:
- how plants survive in the desert
- how plants use and store water when rain is rare.

Did you know?

- A cucumber is nearly all water.
- You can grow desert plants at home in a warm room or a heated glasshouse. They need some water, too!
- We eat plants. We write on them, wear them, sit on them and use them to help us get better!

Plants and seeds

Things to learn
- All plants reproduce.
- Some plants produce seeds. Seeds grow into new plants.

Flowers

Many green plants have flowers. Some are easy to see, but some are not.

Trees have flowers but they may not be brightly coloured. Flowers produce **pollen**. This is carried to another flower when the plant reproduces. Pollen is a fine dust that may be carried by the wind or by an insect.

Humming birds live on nectar from flowers. They also enjoy syrup from feeders.

Bees and pollen

Honeybees carry pollen from flower to flower. The flower attracts them because of its bright colours. At the base of each petal, the flower has a store of sugary **nectar**. The bee drinks the nectar, and pollen is brushed onto its coat. When the bee visits another flower, the pollen is brushed off onto that flower.

Different seeds

- Make a collection of seeds. You will find some in packets for the garden and some in the food cupboard. You might collect some from plants. Be careful – some seeds are harmful or even poisonous. What's the biggest seed that you can find? What is the smallest? Can you name them all?

- Try growing some of your seeds. You can sow small seeds in the earth or **compost**. Bigger seeds can be grown by soaking them in water first. Which plant grows from your different seeds?

Dig deeper

Find out:
- more about flowering plants
- how a sunflower reproduces.

Did you know?

- The seeds in some seedless grapes have no hard casing. That's why you can eat them without spitting out the pips!
- A coconut is a very large seed. The avocado fruit has a large seed, too. Only the Quetzal bird can swallow the seed!

I wonder...

Can a plant make seeds without pollen from another plant?

What have you learned?

- You know that plants are living things.
- You know that we all need plants to live. Plants make food and a gas called oxygen. We use plants in other ways, too.
- You can name a root, a stem, a leaf and a fruit that we eat.
- You know that flowering plants use seeds to reproduce.
- You know how to measure and record the growth of a plant.
- You can use your evidence to predict the growth of a plant.

Find out more about…

- how plants grow – and how water rises up the stem
- plants that grow in very dry places and very wet places.

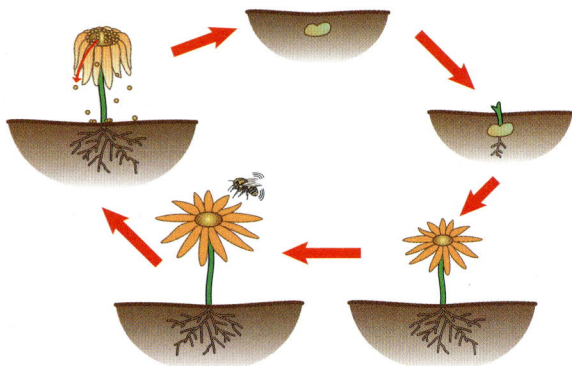

Check-up

Class 3S had a warm classroom. They watered their plants every week. They always left a light on over the plants.

Class 3W had a cold classroom. They often forgot to water their plants. Their classroom was dark at night.

- Whose plants grew better? Explain all the reasons why.
- Write the instructions for a seed packet.

The answer!

Remember the very first question? Shops and garden centres carefully control the heat and light in the glasshouses where the plants are growing. In this way, they can make the plants grow quickly – or slowly. Then the plants are just the right size to put in the garden at the right time.

Unit 3: Characteristics of materials

Imagine you are having a picnic. You have a tin of tuna to eat. But you can't get the lid off. You try a nearby piece of wood, but it **snaps**. You try a plastic knife, but it bends. You carefully try a metal knife. This finally opens the tin. Why was the metal knife best at opening the tin?

What do you know?

- You know the names of some materials.
- You know the properties of some materials.
- Some materials can change their shape.

Words to learn

absorbent	pliable
brittle	property
conductor	rigid
fabric	shiny
flexible	soft
hard	strong
insulator	synthetic
natural	transparent
opaque	

Skills check

Can you...

- measure length?
- change one thing only in a fair test?

Let's find out...

Tyres are made of rubber. Some shoe soles are made of rubber. Why is rubber the best choice of material for these things? The soles of our shoes are not as thick as tyres. Why does the tyre need to be thicker?

Different materials

Things to learn
- All kinds of 'stuff' make materials.
- The same material can do different jobs.
- We call a particular quality of a material – like strength or stretchiness – a property.

Cloth or material?

Imagine a bright blue raincoat with a hood. It's shiny and stretchy. What do you expect it to be made of?

It is made of a **plastic** material called PVC. Most T-shirts are made of **fabric**. Fabrics are one kind of material. So are wood, rubber and metal. List all the materials you can. Which materials are natural? Which are **man-made** or **synthetic**?

PVC is waterproof

What shall I be?

Plastic can be made into lots of different shapes. Your pens are mostly made of plastic. Your pencil case is probably plastic. CDs are plastic and so is the player! You may have plastic trays or a plastic lunch box. List as many other plastic objects as you can.

Properties

Every material has special **properties**. Woods are strong, split easily, burn and usually float. Metals are strong, feel cold and heavy, and make a ringing sound when you hit them. Some materials are **transparent**, like glass. Write down some properties of the materials you listed.

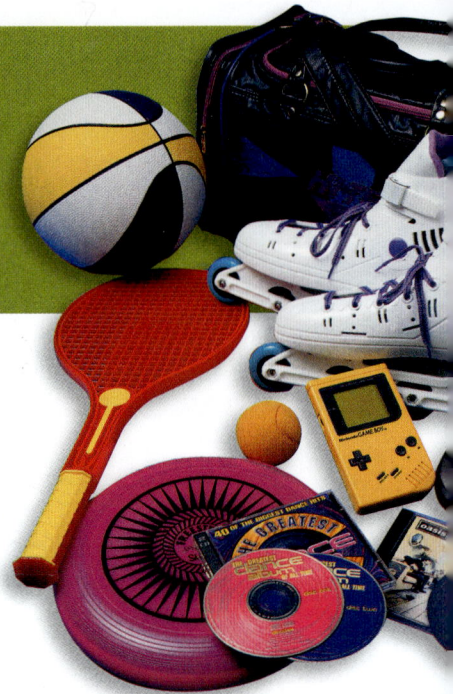

Things to do

All kinds of everything

Your school is made of lots of materials. They are chosen carefully for their job.

- Go around the school and list all the materials you can. Write down what the material is used for.
- Explain how you knew the material. Are some hard to recognize? Which ones? Why?

I wonder...

Look at the surface of your table. What material does it look like? What is it really made from? How do you know? Are you right?

Dig deeper

Find out:
- more about metals as materials why some metals are described as 'precious'.

Some metals are rarer than others

Did you know?

- A white substance called calcium carbonate is one of the most common materials in nature. You can find it in bones, eggshells, chalk, limestone, coral, pearls, shells and **stalactites**!
- Human teeth are almost as hard as rocks!
- Human **thigh** bones are stronger than concrete!
- Aluminium is the commonest metal on Earth, but it is difficult to **extract** from rocks and use.

Things to learn

- Different materials have different properties.
- Different materials can do the same job.
- A material's properties are a guide to what it is best used for.

Cutting edge

The first cutting tool was made from a stone called flint. Its sharp edge was used as a knife. Flint is hard, but it is also **brittle**, so it breaks easily. Better knives were made from **metal**, which is strong and doesn't break as easily as stone. It also stays sharp, but most metals bend. Sometimes we make knives out of plastic. They are cheap but not very strong. Can different materials do the same job? Think about the purpose of different knives.

A chocolate saucepan

Have you ever seen a chocolate saucepan? What material is a saucepan usually made of? Could chocolate do the same job? If you hold a bar of chocolate in your warm hand, it goes **gooey** and melts. Why couldn't a chocolate saucepan be used to heat food?

Chocolate has special properties. It melts in your mouth, at the temperature of your body. That's no good for a saucepan! Saucepans are normally made from metal. Metals are strong and they resist heat, so hot food doesn't melt them!

Things to do

What have you got?

What are the properties of a material? Let's test them.

- Collect lots of different materials. Test how bendy or **flexible** they are. Are they strong? Are they heavy or light? What happens when you **tap** them? Do they feel warm or cold?
- Make a list of all their properties using scientific words.
- How many different properties does your favourite material have?

I wonder...

Could plastic be used to make a cup that holds hot drinks? What properties would the plastic need?

Biographies

Find out:

- what material John Wesley Hyatt invented
- what properties his new material had.

Dig deeper

Find out:

- more about the different kinds and uses of paper
- how writing paper is suited to its job.

Did you know?

- Spider silk is so strong that it is stronger than fine steel wire.
- One type of plastic is stronger than steel. It is called Kevlar. It is used in bullet-proof vests.

Building bridges

Your challenge

- Plan an **experiment** to investigate the best bridge-building materials.
- Explain what you found out using your science knowledge.

What to do

Nadia and Ganesh want to enter a competition for Young Engineers. They have to test the strength of five materials. They have some ideas on how to do it. Which way would you choose? They know that bridges need to be strong. How can they choose the strongest material? They decided to hang weights (scientists call them 'masses') in carrier bags from a bridge of each material to see which holds the most without bending. They will keep all the bridges the same size. Why?

I wonder which material is best for building a bridge?

We could try testing plastic, cardboard, thin card, wood and metal to find out.

We will try bending the materials. Maybe the strongest one won't bend.

We will try stretching the materials. The strongest will not tear or split.

We will tap all the materials. The strongest one won't break.

We will make bridges with the materials and hang masses on them. The strongest won't bend as much.

What you need

- strips of metal, wood, plastic, cardboard and other materials
- masses
- carrier bags

What to check

Now try it yourselves.

- Why do you think you will get good results?
- Which material do you think will be strongest?
- What will happen if a bridge bends or breaks?
- What should you do to be safe?

What did you find?

Nadia and Ganesh put their materials over a gap between two tables. They hung masses from the materials. These are the amounts each material held.

Material	Mass supported (g)
plastic	95
wood	65
cardboard	25
metal	150
thin card	5

- Draw a bar chart of your results or use the Young Engineers' results. Which material was best in this test? How can you tell? Was the test fair?
- If you were building a bridge, which material might you use? What conditions do bridges have to face?

Bridges made from different materials

Can you do better?

Should you wait for the bridge to break? Why might the results be different? How else could you test the bridges? Why might you get the same results if you did the test again? Why do this?

Now predict

- Imagine a bridge-building engineer is coming to your school. Prepare your information. Show her how you are a good researcher of bridge materials. What else could you learn from her?

Comparing materials

Things to learn

- A material can have more than one property.
- Some materials have similar properties.
- Some properties are more useful to us than others.

Prime property

Do you remember the picnic on page 39? Why was the metal knife best at opening the tin? Because metals are strong, the knife was sharp enough to open the tin. Metals are also shiny, but did its shininess help open the tin? Each material has lots of properties and some are more useful than others. Glass is transparent and breaks easily, but which of these properties is important in using glass for windows?

Something in common

Metals are good **conductors** of heat. This means they allow heat to pass through them easily. Other materials may be **insulators** and do not allow heat to pass through easily. Wood and plastic are often used as the insulators of saucepan handles. We don't use wood or plastic for the saucepan itself. Which material do we use? Why?

Name some other materials that are strong, transparent or **rigid**. Name some that do not allow heat to pass through them easily.

Your jeans are not strong enough.

Some materials are stronger than others

I wonder…

Are the wrappers on chocolate bars made of paper or plastic? How can you tell? Try tearing them. You might find a **magnifying glass** useful!

Dig deeper

Find out:
- more about plastic as a material and how useful it is
- why plastic is better than wood and steel for some jobs.

Things to do

Not as tough as boots

Some fabrics are stronger than others. How can you tell which resists wear best? You need to test them.

- Rub a block of wood over the surface of the fabric. Make sure the fabric is flat. What must you keep the same?
- What happens to the fabric after you rub it? This is called 'wear and tear'. Which fabrics wear out?

Did you know?

- Aluminium, glass and paper are materials we recycle or use again, saving lots of energy.
- By reusing or recycling, we can save money, materials and energy.
- In some countries, books are made from animal skins, **reeds** and plastic.

Exploring paper

Your challenge

- Discover which paper absorbs water fastest.
- Keep the test fair.
- Explain what you found out.

Quick! Help me clear up this water. Mum will be cross.

Won't kitchen roll soak it up, though?

Try using toilet paper – there's lots of it.

There's always the art paper you brought home from school!

What to do

One of the children has knocked over some water. Which type of paper will soak it up? Which paper would you tell them to use? Test different types of paper. Which test will show you the fastest absorbing paper?

- Hang each piece of paper in water. Time how long each takes to soak it all up.
- Hang each type of paper in water. See which soaks the liquid furthest up the paper.
- Hang all the pieces of paper in water together. Measure how high the water goes up each paper in one minute.

What you need

- pieces of different paper
- a stopwatch
- a beaker of water
- a measuring jug
- food colouring
- a ruler

What to check

Do your own test. Decide which paper the children should use to mop up a spill.

- Make the test fair. You are changing the paper. What must you keep the same?
- What will you measure?

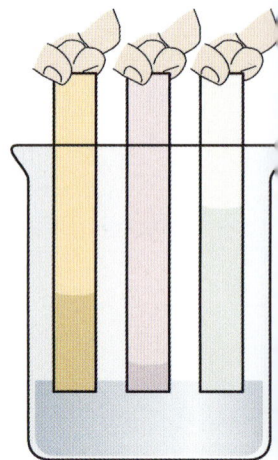

What did you find?

The company that makes SuperSoak kitchen roll also tested how **absorbent** different types of paper are. Here are the results it put on its website.

Paper type	How far the water rose in 1 minute (cm)
Paper tissue	12
Kitchen roll	15
Art paper	8
Writing paper	2
Paper hand towel	10

- Use a computer to draw a bar chart of your results or use the **manufacturer's** results. Which paper absorbs the liquid fastest?
- Which paper would you tell the children to use? Look at that paper carefully and tear one edge. How can you tell it is good at absorbing water?

Can you do better?

Did the brand of paper tissue or kitchen roll make any difference? The manufacturer only tested its own paper. How could its test be fairer?

When does it matter how fast water is absorbed? When does it matter how much?

Now predict

Sadiq works in a science laboratory where the work surface is often wet. He doesn't want his book to get wet.

- What sort of paper should he wrap it in?
- Describe the best sort of paper for the job.

Stretchy materials

Your challenge
- Discover why clothes need to be different sizes.
- Make careful measurements.
- Explain what you found out.

Can you lend me some spare socks, Ammara?

They'll be too big for you. I'm much bigger than you!

They're not for me. My grandma has a hole in hers. She wants to borrow mine! Her feet are much bigger than mine.

Perhaps I should stretch my socks as far as they will go. Then I can give her the longest ones.

Perhaps I should see how far the tops stretch. Then I will know which will go round her ankle.

Maybe I should put masses in them to see how far each sock will stretch.

What to do

Will the socks stretch enough to fit Bushra's grandma? Bushra decided to test some of her socks. Which idea would you try?

What you need
- different pairs of socks
- masses
- 30 cm ruler

What to check

Now try it yourselves.
- What should you keep the same?
- What masses should you use?
- What might give you **clues** before you start?
- How can you tell if the thickness of the socks is important?

What did you find?

Bushra decided to put a 500 g mass in each sock. Ammara would measure them before and after they put each mass in. They would see how much each pair stretched. Bushra came up with these results.

Sock	Length stretched with 500 g mass (cm)
Thick woolly sock	3
Thick sports sock	5
Thin cotton sock	8
Thin sports sock	10
Thin 'pop sock'	12

- Draw a graph using your own or the girls' results. What kind of graph should you draw? You could use a computer to draw it.
- Which pair of socks should Bushra lend to her grandma? How did you decide? What pattern is there in your results? What makes you sure your results are correct?

Can you do better?

How did the length the sock stretched change after each mass was added? What did you measure – the length of the whole sock or how much it stretched?

Now predict

- Rupal is a tracksuit designer. She wants to make a one-size top to fit everyone. How can she test if her fabric will stretch enough?
- Some clothes have Lycra in them. Lycra is an **elastic** fibre. If you tested similar clothes with and without Lycra, what difference would you expect? Why?

What have you learned?

- You know that all kinds of 'stuff' make materials.
- You know that we call a quality of a material – like strength or stretchiness – a property.
- You know that some properties are more useful to us than others.
- You know that we choose materials with properties that are suited to the job they do.
- You know the same material may do different jobs.
- You know different materials may do the same job.
- You know that some materials have similar properties.

Find out more about...

- the right materials for the job
- polymers and **alloys**.

Check-up

Mr Patel wants to build a rabbit **hutch**. The hutch will stay outside all year. It must be easy to keep clean. The rabbit likes gnawing.

- Which materials should Mr Patel use to build the hutch?
- Draw a plan of the hutch for Mr Patel. Explain why you chose the materials.

The answer!

Do you remember the first question? Rubber is a natural substance that is stretchy and springy. The tyres of a car are thicker than our shoes because they get more wear on the roads. A car travels faster and further than our feet!

Unit 4: Rocks and soils

Do you know what's beneath your feet? Under a thin layer of soil there is a crust of rock. This is split into huge pieces called 'plates'. They move slowly against each other and can cause **earthquakes** or **volcanic eruptions**.

What do you know?

- **Rocks** are natural materials.
- We find rocks all over the Earth.
- Rocks come in different sizes and types.
- Rocks have different names.
- We use rocks in different ways.
- Soil is made from worn-down rock mixed with the decaying remains of living things.
- Different soils have different characteristics.

Words to learn

absorbent	marble
chalk	metamorphic
clay	mineral
core	molten
crust	pebble
geologist	permeable
granite	rock
igneous	sand
impermeable	sedimentary
lava	stone
magma	texture
mantle	

Skills check

Can you...

- make careful observations and measurements?
- collect evidence and see how good it is?
- use your evidence to explain what you've found out?
- use your evidence to predict something you don't yet know?

Let's find out...

Eshwar's family has just moved to a new house with a lovely garden, but Eshwar's dad isn't very happy. 'This soil is **waterlogged**. It is heavy clay. It'll take a lot of work before I can grow much in here,' he grumbled. What must Eshwar's dad do to change the soil?

Types of rock

Things to learn

- Rocks are formed in different ways.
- Beneath all surfaces are rocks.
- We use rocks for a variety of jobs.

The Earth

The Earth is made from rock. **Rocks** are the hard parts of the Earth's surface. They cover the Earth's crust – a bit like the peel on an orange. The rocky crust sits on a layer of solid and **molten** rock called the mantle. Inside this is the Earth's **searing**-hot core.

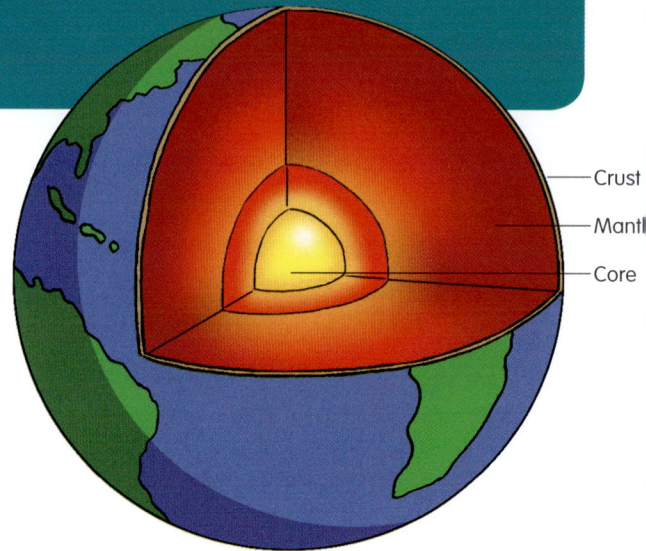

Crust

Mantle

Core

Inside the Earth

What's in a rock

Rocks don't all look the same. They contain minerals that give them different colours and **textures**. Minerals in rocks sometimes form crystals that can be polished and made into jewellery. Some rocks contain metals such as iron, tin or gold. We call these **metallic** rocks 'ores'. Most ores need to be crushed and melted to separate the metals for us to use.

Uses of rocks

In the Stone Age, rocks were used as tools and weapons. Now we use rocks for building houses and roads, and covering roofs. We sometimes use rocks for decoration or art. There's even a rock that we eat! Guess what it is. You shake it on food. How else do we use rocks?

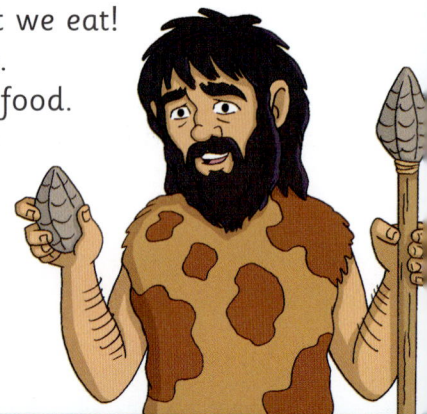

Things to do

Rock feast

Rocks are divided into three main types: **igneous**, **metamorphic** and **sedimentary**. Make your own 'rocks' to eat.

- Igneous rocks, like **basalt** and granite, are formed from the hot rock inside the Earth. Some of the melted rock or lava reaches the surface through volcanoes. Toffee made from sugar boiled in water is like igneous rock.
- Metamorphic rocks, like **slate** and marble, have been changed by great heat or pressure inside the Earth. Food colouring **swirls** make slices of marble cake look like metamorphic rock.
- Sedimentary rocks, like sandstone, are made from bits of other rocks, called sediments. They are washed away by rivers, settle into layers underwater and eventually become solid. Sandwiches with layers of bread, cheese and salad vegetables are arranged like sedimentary rocks.

I wonder…

What does it feel like to be caught up in an earthquake? Some science centres have a shaking 'Earthquake Room'.

Fossil hunter

Use books and websites to find out more about fossils and about a young fossil hunter called Mary Anning who found an ichthyosaur fossil. Fossils are the remains of animals that are preserved in rocks.

Did you know?

- The temperature of the Earth's core is about 6700°C, which is more than 20 times hotter than your kitchen oven!
- We measure the strength of an earthquake using the Richter Scale.
- 'One' on the scale is a slight tremor but 'nine' is a severe quake that could cause enormous damage.

Sorting rocks

Your challenge

● Classify rocks by the way they look.

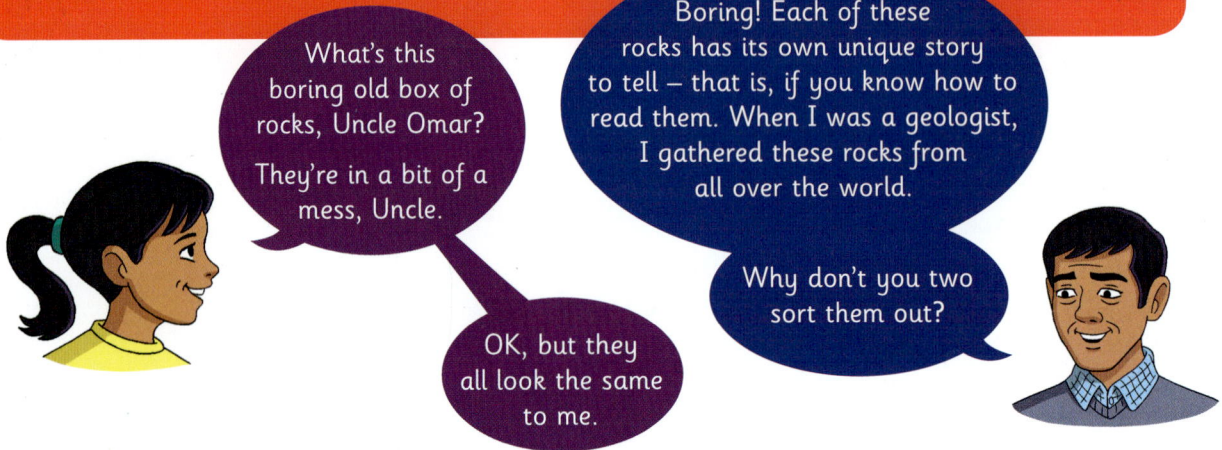

What's this boring old box of rocks, Uncle Omar?

They're in a bit of a mess, Uncle.

OK, but they all look the same to me.

Boring! Each of these rocks has its own unique story to tell – that is, if you know how to read them. When I was a geologist, I gathered these rocks from all over the world.

Why don't you two sort them out?

What to do

Ali and Layla looked very carefully at the collection of rocks. Ali realized that they were all quite different.

Look carefully at your rocks. Think how to group them. Look at the colour or the texture of the surfaces. Are your rocks rough or smooth? Look closely through a magnifying glass or a hand lens. Is each one made of more than one material?

What you need

● a selection of rocks
● a hand lens or magnifying glass

What to check

Now try it yourselves.

● How can you group your rocks?
● Are there any **odd ones out**?
● Some rocks might be bigger than others. Does this matter? Why?

This one has pink crystals in it.

Wow! This one looks like it's made out of seashells.

What did you find?

Uncle Omar told Layla and Ali the name of each rock. They sorted their rocks into three groups like this.

Group 1	Group 2	Group 3
granite	limestone	marble
basalt	chalk	quartzite
sandstone		gneiss

- Layla and Ali then looked up the rocks in a geology book. They decided to move one rock into another group. Which rock do you think they moved and why? What headings should they give to their groups?
- The children made a branching key to help them identify their samples. Here's part of their branching key.

Can you do better?

Make a branching key similar to Layla and Ali's to identify your collection of rocks.

Now predict

Uncle Omar appeared with an old cardboard box. 'I've found a few more for you,' he said. 'Will these fit into your groups too?' Explain how the children will decide which groups the 'mystery rocks' belong to.

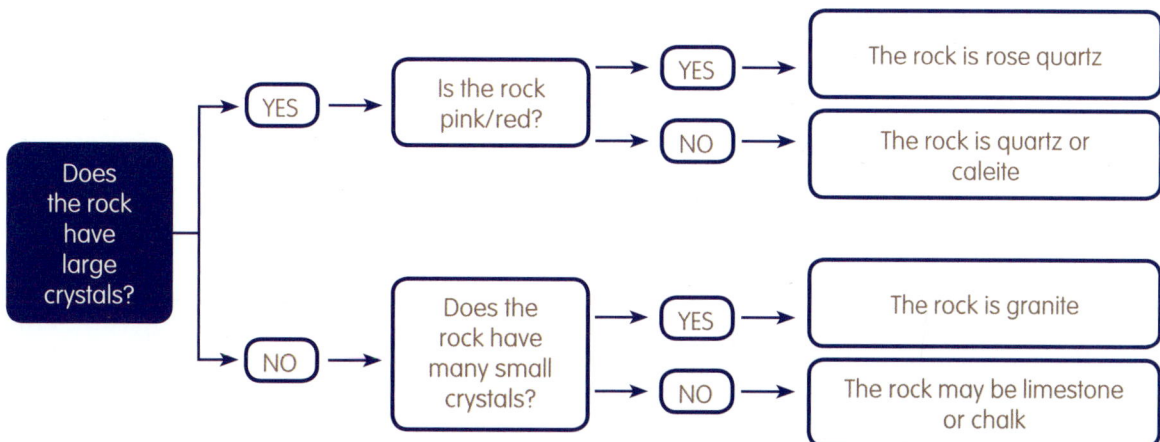

Does the rock have large crystals?
→ YES → Is the rock pink/red?
  → YES → The rock is rose quartz
  → NO → The rock is quartz or calcite
→ NO → Does the rock have many small crystals?
  → YES → The rock is granite
  → NO → The rock may be limestone or chalk

Hard rocks

Your challenge

● Find out which of your rocks is the hardest.

You've sorted these out well, but there are other ways of sorting. How can we do that?

No! They will all sink. Maybe some will soak up water?

We could see whether they float or not.

That's true – chalk does!

We could see if they're rough or smooth, if you can split them easily or how hard they are.

What to do

Are Layla and Ali right? How many ways are there of sorting rocks?

The children decided to do a **scratch** test. They labelled four rocks from 1 to 4. They scratched each one with each of the other rocks in turn. They graded their rocks from the softest (every other rock scratched it) to the hardest (no other rock scratched it). The children rubbed each scratch mark with a soft cloth. Some of the marks came off, others didn't. What did that show?

What you need

● a selection of rocks
● a soft cloth

What to check

Now try it yourselves.

● What are you going to measure?
● How will you make sure that you scratch each rock the same way? How are you going to check and record your results?

What did you find?

Layla and Ali made this table of results, after checking several times that the marks on the rocks were scratches and not bits of the other rock rubbing off. They put a tick when a rock had been scratched.

		Scratched by rock number:			
		1	2	3	4
Rock number	1		x	x	x
	2	✓		x	✓
	3	✓	✓		✓
	4	✓	x	x	

They put all of their results together and made a scale from the softest to the hardest rocks.

softest	3	2	4	1	hardest

- Which rock was scratched by all the other rocks?
- Which rock was the softest? Which was the hardest?
- Make a hardness scale for your results.

Diamond: the hardest rock

Can you do better?

How good is your evidence?

What would you do differently if you tried this again?

Find out about Friedrich Mohs, the German geologist who created a scale of hardness.

Now predict

- Some rocks absorb water. Will they be the harder rocks or the softer ones? How do you know?
- Explain how you could test some rocks to find out which absorb water. Try it!

Types of soil

Things to learn

- Soil covers much of the rocky surface of the Earth.
- Soil is made of tiny pieces of rock and pieces of plants.
- Soil is a mixture of small pieces called particles.
- Different soils have different characteristics.
- Water drains through some soils faster than others.

Wearing down

Rocks are generally **tough**, but over time, **frost**, wind and rain on the rock surface break off small pieces. Gradually the rock is worn away. Many old **gravestones** are 'weathered' like this.

Fertile land

Soil is the layer of the Earth where plants and animals can live and grow. Soil is made up of tiny pieces or particles of weathered rock mixed with the **decaying** remains of plants and animals. Small animals drag bits of plants under the ground and soil bacteria rot these down.

In profile

Soils look and feel different because they are made from different kinds of rock. Some soils have large particles; others have tiny particles. You can find different types of soil in the same field! There are four main types of soil: sandy, clay, chalk and **peat**. All other soils are a mixture of these. Soils from different places are unique. The police can test muddy shoes and car tyres to decide where criminals have been.

Things to do

Analyze some soil

Separate the parts that make up a sample of soil. Different soils will be made of different parts.

- Put some soil in a jar and shake it up with water. Leave it to settle. Soon you will see all of the different parts of your soil separated in layers.
- **Compare** your soil with soil from another area. How are they different?

Dig deeper

Find out:
- more about what farmers can do to their soil to make it more **fertile**.

I wonder...

When it rains, there are puddles in the field next door, but not in my garden. Why is that?

This soil has separated into layers

Did you know?

- Soil forms very slowly. It takes 500 years to make 3 cm of soil.
- The Bamana people of Mali in Africa use black mud as a fabric **dye**. The black and white cloth they make is called 'bogolanfini' or 'mud cloth'.
- A thousand years ago, the Chinese drilled for water using a see-saw with a **chisel** roped to one end. By jumping on and off the **plank**, they dug the chisel into the rock!

Testing soils

Your challenge
● Find out which soil is which.

This is so annoying – I can't remember which field I was in when I lost my grandfather's watch.

It's a family treasure!

Oh dear, these fields are huge – it could be anywhere...

What to do

The students want to help Mr Chopra find his watch. They need to do some detective work. What would you test? You could try all of these – or can you think of something else?

Let's look at the soil on Mr Chopra's boots and match it to a field.

We could sieve it to see the different bits.

Maybe we should see how it feels?

Let's look at the colour of the soil.

We could shake it up with water and see the pattern it makes.

Does it have any leaves or roots in it?

What you need
● a selection of soil samples
● hand lenses or magnifying glasses
● **sieves** with different-sized holes
● clear jars

What to check

Now try it yourselves.

● How many tests will you do?
● What will you keep the same?
● What will you change?
● What will you measure or observe?
● How will you keep the test fair?

Field 1

Field 2

Field 3

Things to do

The students decided to do four different tests to compare the soils. They took samples from each field and compared these with soil from Mr Chopra's boots. They looked at colour, texture, how big the bits or 'particles' were and how the soils separated in water. Here are their results.

Sample from	Colour	Texture	Size of particle
Mr Chopra's boots	dark brown	crumbly	large
Field 1	red brown	gritty	small
Field 2	dark brown	crumbly	large and stony
Field 3	dark brown	sticky	powdery

They drew pictures of how the soils had separated.

- Which field had Mr Chopra been working in when he lost his watch?
- How do you know?

Can you do better?

How good is your evidence?

How many soils could you match this way?

What would you do differently if you tried this again?

Now predict

- Think of other ways the students could test their soils.
- Would the results be the same if they took samples from the edges of the fields rather than the middle?
- The soil in one of the fields felt sticky – why do you think that was?

Soil and water

Your challenge

- Find out which soil **drains** the quickest.

I have to plant these seeds in 'well-drained' soil. What does that mean?

What to do

Decide what to measure and how to record your results. Here's what Tariq did. What do you think?

Tariq made some funnels from empty pop bottles. He lined them with soft paper then filled each funnel with a different type of soil. He used sand, clay, **gravel** from his fish tank and some potting compost. He also tested the soil from his garden.

He measured water and poured the same amount in each funnel. He watched to see which soil the water drained through the fastest.

Well, plants won't grow properly if the soil is too wet. You must plant them where the heavy rain will drain away.

What to check

Now try it yourselves.

- What will you measure?
- Will you repeat the experiment?
- Why is this a good idea?
- How will you record your mixtures?
- How will you keep the test fair?

What you need

- funnels or the tops of pop bottles
- different soils or sand, clay and compost mixtures
- rulers
- a measuring jug
- a seconds timer
- soft paper

Things to do

Tariq recorded how long it took for the water to drain through. Tariq stopped timing when the water stopped dripping. Here is the table of his results.

Soil type	Time for 10ml of water to drain through
sand	1 minute 14 seconds
clay	more than 8 minutes
compost	2 minutes 34 seconds
gravel	6 seconds
garden soil	2 minutes 55 seconds

Tariq found that the gravel was the most **permeable** material. The clay was the most **impermeable** material.

- Make a chart of your own or Tariq's results. You could use a computer program to help you.
- Which of your soils was most permeable?
- Which drains the slowest?

Can you do better?

How good is your evidence?

What would you do differently if you did this experiment again?

How useful do you think Tariq's results are?

Now predict

- Tariq found out that water drained fastest through gravel, but he decided not to plant his seeds in gravel. Why do you think that was?
- What sort of soil would you tell him to use? Why?

What have you learned?

- You know that rock is beneath the surface of the Earth.
- You know that different rocks have different properties.
- You know that some rocks soak up water.
- You know that some rocks are harder than others.
- You know that different rocks are used for different purposes.
- You know that soil is made of broken-down rock and decaying plants.
- You know that different soils have different properties.
- You know that water drains through some soils faster than others.

Find out more about...

- other Earth products that we use, such as metal ores, natural gas, coal and oil.

This is the Rock of Gibraltar

Check-up

Nafisa and Yassmin were walking along a beach when they saw something sparkling in the sand. Nafisa thought that she'd found a diamond. Yassmin was sure it was just glass.

- Think of one test they could do to find out who was right.
- Further along the beach they came to a rock pool. The seawater drained away through the beach sand, but stayed in pools in the rocks. Explain why.

The answer!

Do you remember the question about Eshwar's dad and his new garden? The soil was waterlogged. It was heavy clay. Most plants won't grow well if their roots are in water all of the time. The particles in the soil must be big to allow air in and create spaces for the water to drain away. Eshwar's dad could add sand and gravel to the soil. That will make more spaces for air and drainage.

Unit 5: Magnets and springs

You can't see a force but you can see what forces do. Forces are at work all the time, even when you're sitting still or sleeping. Magnetism is a force and so is **gravity**. Just think what life would be like without gravity!

Skills check

Can you...

- make careful observations and measurements?
- collect evidence and decide how good it is?
- use evidence to explain what you've found out?

What do you know?

- Forces are pushes and pulls.
- Forces can be large or small.
- Forces can be measured.
- Forces act in particular directions.
- Forces can speed things up or slow them down, make them start moving, stop, change direction or even change shape.

Let's find out...

Could you jump over a fence in spring-heeled boots? Imagine your shoes had springs on the heels. You might bounce on them – but could you jump very high?

Words to learn

alloy	forcemeter	pole
attract	horseshoe	repel
bar	limit	spring
compress	magnet	
elastic	magnetic	
extend	magnetism	
field	newton	
force	non-magnetic	

Magnetic forces

Things to learn
- There are forces between magnets.
- Magnets can attract and repel each other.

What is a magnet?

A magnet attracts some metals. It attracts other magnets. Magnets are mostly made from iron or **alloys** of iron. Magnets can **attract** objects that are magnetic. Magnets can **repel** other magnets.

The area where a magnet has an effect is called a magnetic **field**.

North and south poles

The two ends of a magnet are called the north and south **poles** because magnets were first used as a compass to help travellers find their way. One pole of a free-moving magnet always points north. How could you test this? How could you find the poles of an unmarked magnet?

Put the north poles of two bar magnets close to each other. Feel them repel each other. What happens with two south poles? How about north and south? What happens when you put magnets side by side? Does the shape of the magnet make a difference?

Magnets come in all shapes and sizes. Where are the poles of these magnets?

Very attractive

We use magnets every day. Knives can 'stick' to a magnet on a knife rack because they are made of a **magnetic** material. Why can't you stick a wooden spoon on in the same way?

Things to do

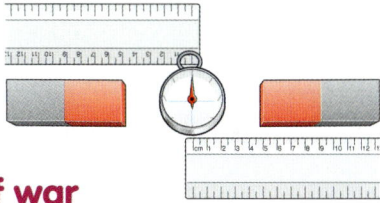

Tug of war

A compass has a free-moving magnetic needle. It lines up with the Earth's magnetic force lines. If you put a magnet near a compass, you can move the needle away from its natural north–south position.

- Play a game of **tug of war**. Line up the needle point on a compass to north. Take two bar magnets and place their south poles near the east and west sides of the compass. What happens?
- Gently move one magnet nearer the compass – what happens?
- Try this again with different magnets.

Fly a plane

You can use magnets to perform 'magic' tricks.

- Tape one end of a thread to your desk and tie the other to a paper clip. Cut an aeroplane shape out of tissue paper and put this onto the paper clip.
- Use a magnet to make your plane fly – without touching the paper clip!

Dig deeper

Find out:
- how many different ways we use magnets.

Did you know?

- A scientist called Peter the Pilgrim wrote about the poles of a magnet over 700 years ago.
- The strongest magnets are **ceramic**. They are made from metal powders heated together with other non-metals under very high pressure.

Magnets can even lift and move some trains!

I wonder...

Electricity can be used to make a type of magnet called an electromagnet. We can switch electromagnets on and off. Where might this be useful?

Magnetic materials

Your challenge
- Explore how some materials are magnetic and some are not.
- Plan a fair test.

I think all metal things are magnetic.

No, they're not. Only some metals are magnetic.

Use a magnet to test things around the classroom. Be careful not to test anything electrical or your watch!

It's not fair! My magnet's smaller than yours!

What to do

Gather together all the things you are going to test and sort them into two groups. Predict which objects are magnetic and will be attracted to a magnet, which are non-magnetic and won't be attracted to a magnet. Test your materials with a magnet – were you right?

What you need
- a selection of safe objects to test
- magnets

What to check

What do you think will happen?

- Do you think all of the object will be magnetic or just part of it?
- What will you record?

What did you find?

Class 3 were surprised by some of their results. This is what they predicted.

Magnetic	scissors, paper clips, aluminium drink can, metal pencil sharpener, stainless steel spoon, copper coin, cooking foil
Not magnetic	rubber, pencil, plastic ruler, card, cotton wool

But this is what they discovered.

Magnetic	scissors, paper clips, metal pencil sharpener
Not magnetic	rubber, pencil, plastic ruler, card, cotton wool, cooking foil, copper coin, stainless steel spoon, aluminium drink can

- Present your results or Class 3's results. Use a computer program to help you.
- Can you write a general rule about magnetic materials?

Wait a moment – this new copper coin is attracted to a magnet but this older one isn't.

Can you do better?

Did you get results like those of Class 3? Some metals look exactly the same but some are attracted by a magnet and some aren't. How are they different?

Now predict

- Class 3 want to collect aluminium cans so that they can be recycled and reused. How could a magnet help them?

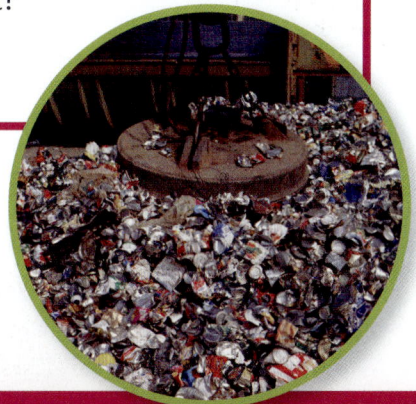

Strength of magnets

Your challenge
- Find which is the strongest magnet.
- Make careful observations and measurements.
- Plan a fair test.

I think the biggest magnet is the strongest.

Nafisa says the heaviest one is the strongest.

Ahmed thinks they're all the same.

Omar says the weakest will be the one covered in plastic.

What to do
Who do you think is right? Decide how to measure your magnet's strength. Look at these different tests. You could do all of these.

We'll see how many paper clips the magnet can attract.

We're going to find out how many sheets of paper the magnet will work through.

We're going to measure how close the magnet has to be before it attracts a paper clip.

Let's see how much water the magnet will attract through.

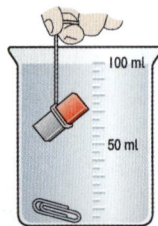

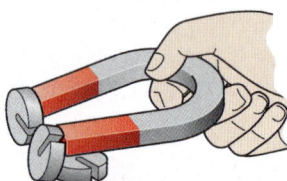

We're going to find the heaviest object a magnet can lift.

What you need
- paper clips
- different magnets
- rulers or measuring tapes
- measuring cylinder or beaker of water

What to check
Now try it yourselves. What do you think will happen?

- What are you going to measure?
- Will you always use the same pole of each magnet? Is that fair?

What did you find?

Shameena's group hung paper clips onto each magnet to test its strength. Their results looked like this.

Type of magnet	Number of paper clips held in a chain
Small round	12
Doughnut shaped	10
Plastic-covered bar	8
Horseshoe	8
Long bar	6
Magnetic strip	4

● Draw a chart of your own results or those of Shameena's group. Use a computer program to help you.

● Shameena's group predicted the biggest magnet would be the strongest. They were wrong – one of the smaller magnets held the most paper clips. How could they make sure their results are correct?

Can you do better?

How good is your evidence?

What would you do differently if you tried this again?

Is there another test you could do to check your results?

Is it true to say that smaller magnets are always stronger?

Now predict

● Shameena has a collection of magnets on her fridge door. She's noticed that sometimes the notes and magnets slip down the fridge door. Why does this happen?

Stretching and squeezing

Things to learn

- Springs are used in a variety of ways.
- Springs can be squashed or stretched, pushed or pulled.
- A squashed spring pushes up with the same amount of force that squashes it down.
- A stretched spring pulls back with the same amount of force that stretches it.
- If you stretch a spring too far, it will not go back into shape.

Springs

Springs are all around us – most are made from a **spiral** of metal. There are big springs on trampolines and tiny springs in door locks. Springs are in cars and trucks, on bikes, in toys, computers, clocks, and even some pens. How many more springs can you think of?

That's the limit

You can't stretch a spring forever! When you compress or **squeeze** a spring, you push the particles it is made from closer together. When you let it go, they jump apart. An **elastic** band is a bit like a spring. If you extend or stretch it, you can feel the force pulling back on your hands. If you let go, it will spring back to its original shape. But if you keep on stretching, it will not go back into shape. It may snap! This is its '**elastic limit**'.

Watch out!

Before batteries, all watches were 'wound up' or ran on springs. In the seventeenth century, Robert Hooke invented a clock spring, small enough to fit in a wristwatch. Before that, the smallest portable clock had been the size of your **fist**!

Things to do

Measure a force

Household scales use springs to measure weight. The spring has a pointer on it. When the spring is squeezed, the pointer moves along a scale. This tells us how heavy the object is. You can also measure weight by stretching a spring.

A **forcemeter** has a spring inside it. As you pull the spring, it pulls back. It moves a pointer on a scale. The bigger the force, the more you stretch the spring. We measure force in **newtons**.

- Make your own forcemeter using cardboard, paper fasteners, a yoghurt pot and an elastic band.

I wonder...

Can hard things be springy too?

Did you know?

- The world record **bungee jump** was from a helicopter. The bungee stretched from 250 m to over 600 m.
- A newton is a unit of force named after Isaac Newton. One newton pulls down with the force of a medium-sized apple.

Paper frog

Springs work because all objects change shape when they are pulled or pushed. They get their shape back once the pull or push is removed, unless they have been tested beyond their elastic limit!

- Fold paper to make an origami frog with a **zigzag** paper spring. How far can it jump? If you compress the spring lightly, will it jump as far as when you squash the spring right down?
- What happens if you change the number of zigzags in the spring?

Exploring springs

Your challenge

- Explore how far a spring can stretch.
- Measure and record accurately.
- Communicate your results to others.

What to do

Carefully cut out a paper spiral. Fix it to a table edge or to a chair on top of a table. Measure the length of the **uncoiled** spiral and record the length. You may need one paper clip for your first measurement. Why?

Add paper clips to the spiral one at a time and record the length each time.

When your spiral will not stretch any more, draw a graph of your results. Put the number of paper clips on the x-axis and the length of the spring on the y-axis.

How can you have a spring made from paper?

Should I hang my spring from the middle or the end?

I don't know. I'm going to cut mine out carefully.

Does it matter where we put the paper clips?

What you need

- a paper spiral
- scissors
- sticky tape
- paper clips
- a measuring stick or tape measure
- graph paper

What to check

- When does the spiral spring stop stretching? Why?
- What distance are you going to measure?
- Where will you hang your paper clips? Will it make a difference where you hang them?
- Does it matter if you use a different type of paper or a different-shaped spiral?

What did you find?

Class 3 took averages of all their results and put them into a table. It looked like this.

Number of paper clips	Length of spring (cm)
0	21
1	23
2	27
3	30
4	32
5	33
6	34
7	34
8	34
9	34
10	34

- Draw a graph of your results or Class 3's results. Use a computer program to record your results and to draw a graph.
- What does your graph tell you? Did the spring stretch by the same amount each time a paper clip was added? Why did the spring stop stretching? When you took all the paper clips off, did the spring go back to its original length?

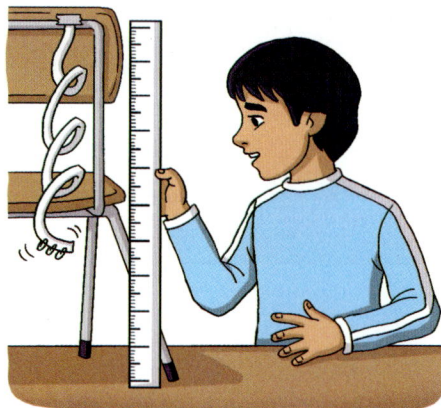

Can you do better?

Did you always measure between the same two points?

What pattern did you notice in the results?

Class 3's teacher asked for an average of the results for each group. Why do you think he did this?

What would you do differently if you tried this again?

Now predict
- Make spirals which are thinner and thicker.
- Do you think both will have the same elastic limit?

Spring power

Your challenge
- Find out which is the springiest elastic band.
- Make careful observations and measurements.
- Plan a fair test.

What to do

When you wind up an elastic band, you are storing force or energy in it. When you unwind it, you are releasing that energy. Class 3 wanted to find out how far forwards an elastic band could power a cotton reel. Follow their instructions to find out.

First make a cotton-reel tank. Thread your elastic band through the hole in a cotton reel and loop one end over a matchstick. Hold it still with sticky tape.

What you need
- cotton reels
- elastic bands
- large beads
- matchsticks
- short pencils
- metre rulers
- sticky tape

Then thread a bead onto the other end of the elastic band and push a pencil through the loop of the elastic.

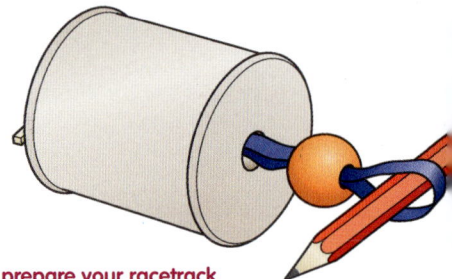

Finally, prepare your racetrack by laying out a metre ruler and a start line. Wind up the elastic band using the pencil. Count the winds.

What to check
- What are you going to measure?
- How will you keep the test fair?
- What will you do if your tank doesn't move in a straight line?
- How many elastic bands will you test?

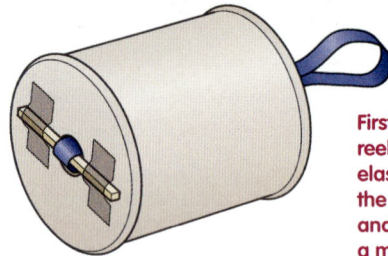

Place the cotton-reel tank on the track, with the pencil tip touching the work surface. Carefully let the cotton-reel tank go. Measure how far it travels.

What did you find?

Class 3 presented their results in a table. It looked like this.

Number of full turns of the pencil	Distance travelled (cm)
5	3
10	5
15	12
20	20
25	29
30	38

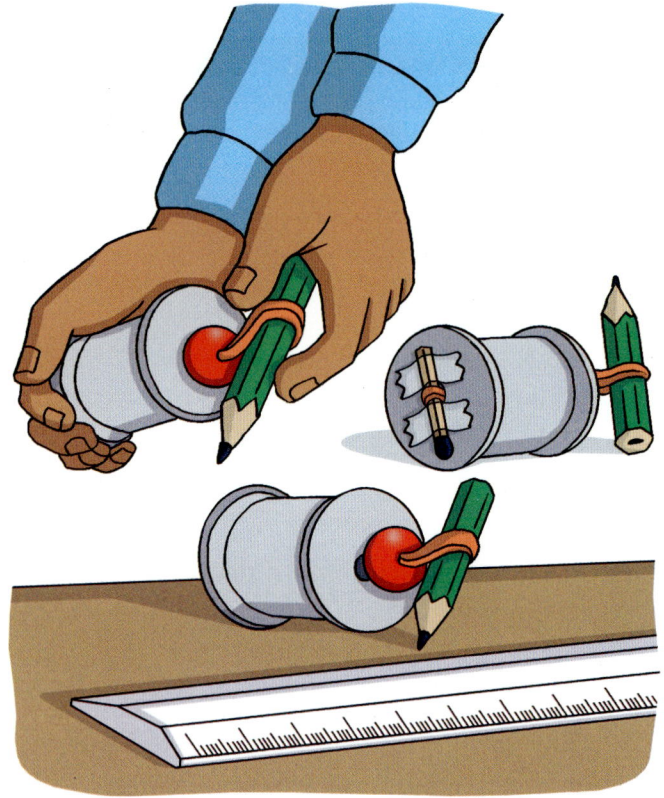

- Draw a chart of your own results or those of Class 3. Use a computer program to help you.
- Can you write a general rule about the number of turns needed to move the tank a certain distance?

Can you do better?

How did the elastic band change as it was wound over and over?

How did you make sure the length of the pencil didn't change?

What else did you control?

Now predict

- Predict from these results how far the tank would travel after 40 turns, or after 50.
- Class 3 tested different elastic bands – thicker, thinner, longer and shorter ones. They made a different results table for each elastic band they used. Predict what they discovered.

What have you learned?

- You know that magnets and springs are very useful in many different ways.
- You can describe the action of forces on magnets and springs.
- You know that you cannot stretch a spring beyond its elastic limit.
- You know how to measure a force.
- You know some materials that are magnetic and some that are not.

Find out more about...

- how magnets can make iron and steel magnetic
- how electricity can make iron and steel magnetic.

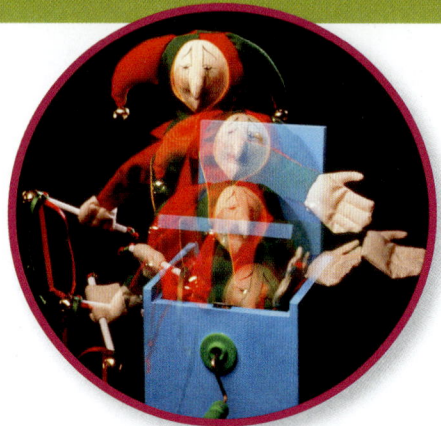

Check-up

Antwan and Raheem were having a **catapult** competition. Antwan's catapult had a long, thin piece of elastic attached to it. Raheem's elastic was short and thick. They both pulled back their elastic the same distance and fired a ball of **scrunched-up** paper at a target.

- Whose paper ball went furthest?
- Explain the reasons why.
- Design a toy that uses magnetic forces to move.

The answer!

Do you remember the question about spring-heeled boots? Sadly, you could not jump over the fence. If you pull a spring, it pulls back. If you squash a spring – by jumping on it – it will push back with the force you put in. So you will not jump much higher than usual.

Unit 6: Friction

Friction happens when two surfaces move against each other. It lets us walk without slipping and sliding. It's the reason things don't slip out of our hands.

What do you know?
- Forces are pushes and pulls.
- We measure forces in newtons (N).
- Forces act in particular directions.
- We can't always see forces but we can measure them and observe what they do.
- Forces can make objects move, go faster or slower, change direction or even change shape.
- Friction is a force that slows things down.

Skills check
Can you...
- make careful observations and measurements?
- collect evidence and see how good it is?
- use your evidence to explain what you've found out?
- use your evidence to predict?

Words to learn
air resistance
forcemeter
friction
lubricant
lubrication
streamlined
streamlining
surface area
water resistance

Let's find out...

Haniya's grandad slipped on his bathroom floor tiles. He wasn't hurt but he wanted his home to be made safer for him.

Haniya and her mum are changing things in the bathroom and kitchen so that nothing will be too slippery. What changes could they make?

What is friction?

Get a grip

Friction is caused by two surfaces moving against each other. As one surface passes over the other, they grip. This slows the movement down.

If the surface area is very big or the surfaces are very similar, there will be more friction and things will move very slowly.

How friction works

Even surfaces we think are perfectly smooth have a rough surface. If we look at them through a powerful microscope, we can see **troughs** and **ridges**. These troughs and ridges catch against each other and slow things down.

Slipping and sliding

Friction helps us to walk. If our feet didn't grip the floor, we'd slip as if we were walking on ice. Have you ever slid across a polished floor in your socks? Is it easier or harder than sliding with trainers on? Shoes have a textured sole, called a 'tread', to stop you sliding.

Wheels have treads too. The tyres on a mountain bike or the caterpillar tracks on a digger have deep treads to grip on rough ground.

Skate away

Sledges need to slide across the snow easily. They have narrow runners to reduce the surface in contact with the snow. Skates also have narrow blades to reduce the friction with the ice.

Marbles

- Put **marbles** in a bowl. Using only two fingers, see how many marbles you can move to another bowl in a minute. Now add some cooking oil to the marbles and try to move them back. How many can you move in a minute this time?
- Wipe up any spilt oil from the floor to avoid an accident.

Exploring

Oil and water are both examples of lubricants. We use lubrication to reduce friction between moving surfaces.

Dig deeper

Find out:
- where friction is useful or a nuisance and how we can reduce friction.

Did you know?

- Polar bears have fur on the soles of their feet to help them grip the ice.
- Watchmakers use tiny '**jewels**' to reduce friction between the moving parts in watches.

Things to do

Fiction and heat

- Lots of friction causes heat. Campers know that the friction caused by rubbing two sticks together can sometimes cause enough heat to light a fire.
- Rub your hands together really quickly. The friction between your palms should create heat. Now do it under a running tap. What happens? Why do you think this is?

I wonder...

Why do the brakes on a bike work better on a dry day than on a wet one?

Measuring forces

Your challenge

- Explore the forces needed to move an object across a surface.
- Plan a fair test.
- Measure and record forces in newtons.

Haniya watched her brother pull his toy truck. The more blocks he put in his truck, the harder it was to make it move. Haniya wondered why this was. She decided to investigate.

What to do

Haniya found an empty dish and tied it to a forcemeter. She put the dish on the kitchen table and gently pulled on the forcemeter until the dish moved. She wrote down the force needed to make the dish move.

Haniya added five marbles to the dish to make it heavier. Each time she added more marbles, she noted how much force was needed to move the dish.

What to check

Now try it yourselves.

- Haniya measured the force when the dish first started to move. Will you do the same?
- What surface will you do the experiment on?
- Use a forcemeter if you have one.
- What do you think will happen?

What you need

- a plastic dish
- string
- a forcemeter
- several masses or marbles
- several surfaces, such as wood, card, carpet, sandpaper or plastic

What did you find?

Haniya made a table of her results. It looked like this.

Number of marbles	Force needed to start dish moving (N)
0 (empty)	0.2
5	1.2
10	2.2
15	3.2
20	4.2
25	5.2
30	6.2
35	7.2

Haniya noticed that with more marbles in the dish, the reading on her forcemeter was higher. She thought that a heavier dish needed more force to start it moving along the surface of the table.

- Use a spreadsheet to record your results. Then plot them on a line graphs. Put the number of marbles or the mass on the x-axis. Plot the force needed to move the dish on the y-axis.

Can you do better?

How good is your evidence? How could you improve it?

Can you make a general rule about your results?

Now predict

- What do you think would happen if Haniya changed the container she used? Does the size of the container make a difference to how much force is needed to move it?
- Do you think her results would be different if she did the experiment on the carpet? Why?
- Haniya took a few marbles out of the dish. What do you think happened?

Slippery surfaces

Your challenge

- Find out which surface is the most slippery.

My car's faster than yours. It's got bigger tyres.

That's not what's important. My car will win because it's lighter.

But it depends what you race them on.

Why don't we try to find out the best racing surface first?

What to do

The students in Mr Khan's class were having a race. They decided to find out what would be the best racing surface. They had to decide what to measure and how to record their results. Look at what the students thought. What do you think?

That's a wooden plank. Let's cover it with different materials to see which is the most slippery.

We all need the same equipment.

I'm going to tilt this plank up until the wood block starts to move. Then I'll measure how high the end was when the block moved.

Are we measuring from when it first starts to move or from when it gets to the bottom of the plank?

What you need

- a wooden block to act as your vehicle
- a **ramp** or plank
- materials to cover your plank's surface: carpet, card, **bubble wrap**, rubber, foil
- a metre ruler
- books or bricks to support the end of the plank

What to check

Now try it yourselves.

- What are you going to measure?
- Is it fair?
- Are you only changing one thing?
- What do you think will happen?

What did you find?

The students stopped adding bricks when the wooden block first began to slip down the slope. They changed the surface of the slope and repeated their experiment using the same wooden block. They recorded their results in a table.

Surface of ramp	Height in bricks before the block moved
Wood	3
Card	2
Carpet	4
Felt	5
Sandpaper	2

- Make a chart of your results. Use a computer program to help you.
- Which was the surface with the most friction? Which was the most slippery? Why do you think that was?

Can you do better?

How good is your evidence? What would happen if you lubricated the ramp? What would you use?

Now predict

Mr Khan decided to have a 'Snail Grand Prix'. He gave a prize to the car that reached the finish line last on a **tilted** ramp. The students could use any surface to cover the ramp and the tyres on the toy cars.

- What do you think the students chose for the ramp and tyres?
- What do you think the winning car had on its tyres?
- If you have a light gate for your computer, use it to check which car moved first.

Different forces

Things to learn

- Friction is a force that exists between moving surfaces.
- Friction exists in liquids and gases too.
- Air resistance is a force that slows objects moving through air.
- Water resistance is a force that slows objects moving through water.

Forces all around

We live at the bottom of a sea of air. We are surrounded by **invisible** air. It presses down on us all the time. We can feel its force when the wind blows or when we move through it. We call this force **air resistance**.

We feel the force of the air when the wind blows

Slowing down

A **parachute** slows down as it falls through the air because the air rubs against it. A parachute with a big **canopy** will fall slower than one with a small canopy. This is because there is a bigger **surface area** in contact with the air and so there is more air resistance.

Streamlined shapes

Objects that have large, flat shapes meet a lot of resistance in water. Fish and marine mammals have pointed, slim body shapes to cut through the water. Their shapes reduce the **water resistance** that slows them down. We call these shapes **streamlined**. Streamlining is important in air too. The fastest sports cars have narrow, pointed, streamlined shapes. The air passes quickly over them and reduces the amount of air resistance.

Things to do

Fly a kite

- Make some different-shaped kites and fly them on a windy day. Which kites are the easiest to control? What difference does the size of the kite make? Can you feel how hard you have to pull on your kite against the air pushing it up?

A simple wind gauge

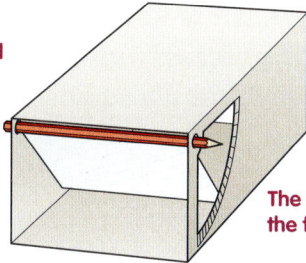

The wind blows the flap

Windy weather

Sailors need to know the strength of the wind to help them sail.

- Find out about Admiral Beaufort and his wind scale.
- Make a 'wind gauge' to measure the force of the wind. Are your results the same as the local weather forecast?
- Use a digital recorder to record and play your own weather forecast.

I wonder...

Why are submarines torpedo-shaped and not cubes or spheres?

Dig deeper

Find out:
- more about friction in air and water
- how parachutes work.

Did you know?

- The first kites were made 3000 years ago in China from silk and **bamboo**
- In June 2000, a skydiver made a parachute jump from a height of 2 miles using a triangular-shaped parachute designed in 1485! Lots of scientists thought it wouldn't work but he glided to Earth quite safely!

Testing spinners

Your challenge

● Find out which is the best spinner.

What's this?

It's a flying seed from a sycamore tree. We used to call them 'helicopters' when I was little. I wonder how it got here? I can't see any trees around.

What to do

The students cut out their own spinners based on the sycamore seed they found. They thought about all of the ways they could change them.

You could try all of these – or can you think of something else?

What you need

● spinner template
● scissors
● different sorts of paper
● paper clips
● a stopwatch or seconds timer
● a measuring tape

What to check

Now try it yourselves.

● What are you going to keep the same?
● What are you going to change?
● What are you going to measure or observe?
● How are you going to keep the test fair?
● What do you think will happen?

Let's make one from paper.

I'm going to make mine out of tissue paper.

I think it would be better if it was bigger.

It needs to be heavier.

I'm going to make the wings longer.

I want mine to be yellow.

What did you find?

The students changed the paper the spinner was made from. They thought that the slower it fell, the 'better' it was. They dropped their spinners from the same height each time. They measured how long they took to hit the ground. The students drew a table of their results.

Spinner material	Time taken (seconds)
Writing paper	3.2
Tissue paper	2.0
Thin card	1.5
Newspaper	3.6
Magazine paper	4.4

The students weren't sure that they were using the best materials to make spinners. They noticed that the tissue-paper spinner collapsed. They thought that maybe that wasn't fair. When they tried the magazine paper, their teacher walked past and made a **draught**. Maybe that wasn't fair?

- Can you tell the students where they went wrong with their investigation?

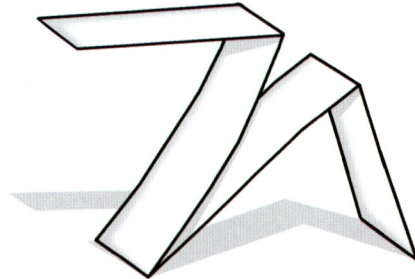

Can you do better?

What would you do if your results didn't seem quite right?

Now predict

- What other ways could the students test their spinners?
- Would the results be the same if they added paper clips to the spinners to make them heavier?
- What would happen if they dropped them from a higher place?
- Do you think the size of the spinner matters? Why?
- What is it about flying seeds that makes them spread everywhere?

Exploring friction

Your challenge

- Find out which shapes are the most streamlined.

What to do

Decide what you're going to measure and how you'll record your results. Here's what Omar said to Rasheed. What do you think?

What you need

- a long tube or plastic pop bottle with the top cut off
- very small pieces of plasticine – all the same size
- wallpaper paste or clear liquid soap
- thread
- a stopwatch or seconds timer

What to check

Now try it yourselves.

- What are you going to measure?
- How many times will you repeat the investigation?
- Why is this a good idea?
- What shapes will you try?
- How will you keep the test fair?
- What do you think will happen?

Why is it I'm the fastest in school at **butterfly** and you can still beat me?

It's because I swim front crawl. It's a more streamlined stroke. I'm bound to be faster.

What do you mean, streamlined?

If you're a streamlined shape, like an arrow, you can move through water faster than if you're all spread out.

So if you spread out your arms and hands wide, you wouldn't cut through water as easily as if you kept your arms and legs close?

That's right. If you keep your body in a line you'll move faster too.

What did you find?

The boys tested the idea. They timed how long it took different plasticine shapes to fall to the bottom of a bottle of paste. This is the table of their results.

Shape of plasticine	Time taken (seconds)
Flat square	2.3
Dome	2.6
Sphere	1.9
Sausage	1.5
Torpedo	1.7

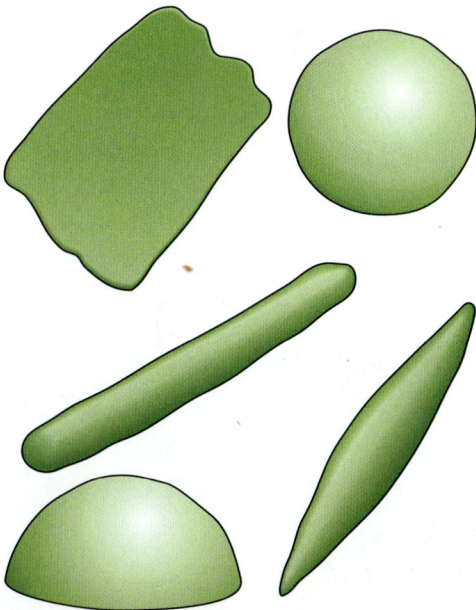

- Make a chart of your results. Use a computer program to help you.
- If you have a digital video recorder, record your results.
- Make a PowerPoint presentation of your investigation.

Can you do better?

How good is your evidence?

What would you do differently if you did this investigation again?

Now predict

The boys made sure all of the plasticine pieces weighed the same. But they were surprised by their results. They thought the torpedo shape would be quickest.

- Why do you think they were wrong? Why do you think the **dome** shape was the slowest? Can you think of any other shapes to try?

What have you learned?

- You know that friction is a force that slows moving objects down.
- You know that lubrication reduces friction between solid surfaces.
- You know that air resistance is a force that slows things moving in air.
- You know that water resistance is a force that slows things moving in water.
- You know that streamlined shapes can reduce air and water resistance.

Find out more about...

- why a space shuttle gets so hot as it re-enters the Earth's atmosphere
- why a space shuttle doesn't get hot as it travels through outer space
- how a space shuttle is slowed down as it lands.

Check-up

Farida is competing in an endurance bike race. She has to ride round and round a track for 5 miles! She is very fit and knows that she will be able to keep going. But she thinks that air resistance might slow her down.

- What should she wear to cut down her air resistance?

The answer!

Do you remember the question about Haniya's grandad? Smooth surfaces, particularly when they are lubricated with something like water, can become very slippery and dangerous. Haniya's grandad can increase the friction by keeping the surfaces dry. He could also use low-friction materials such as rubber mats to help increase his grip.

What do you know?

- Think about these statements.
- Which do you know? Which have you learned?

- I know that all animals eat, drink, move, grow and reproduce.
- I know that humans have five senses.
- I know that exercise is important for a healthy lifestyle.
- I have learned to identify different types of food and teeth.
- I have learned about what I eat and drink and how to keep my teeth healthy.
- I know that animals need food and water to grow.
- I can make observations of toothpaste rubbing off stains and compare different results.
- I have learned to use a table to record my results.
- I know that we need a healthy diet to live and grow.
- I have learned to describe the components of a healthy diet.
- I have learned to compare different toothpastes fairly.
- I have learned to name and explain the functions of different teeth.
- I have learned to explain why different food groups are essential to our health.
- I know that to make the test fair, I must use the same toothpaste and pressure each time.
- I have learned to record my results on a bar chart and explain what it means.
- I have learned to relate my results to what I know about keeping teeth healthy.

What do you know?
- Think about these statements.
- Which do you know? Which have you learned?

- I have learned to describe one or more differences between two things.
- I have learned to describe one or more similarities between two things.
- I have learned to separate objects into two groups on the basis of a rule.
- I have learned to use a branching key to separate four or more objects.
- I have learned to prepare and use a branching key to sort objects using yes/no questions.
- I have learned to describe a plant.
- I have learned to say what I observe.
- I have learned to say what plants need in order to grow.
- I have learned to make and record regular observations of my plant.
- I have learned to explain why plants need water, warmth and light to grow.
- I have learned to make and record regular measurements of my plant.
- I know that plants and animals are living things.
- I know that plants use water and carbon dioxide to make their own food.
- I know that not watering a plant, while keeping all other conditions the same, is a fair test of the effect of watering to the plant.
- I know that flowers and plants use seeds to reproduce.

Unit 3: Characteristics of materials checklist

What do you know?
- Think about these statements.
- Which do you know? Which have you learned?

- I have learned to describe an object by colour and texture.
- I have learned to say what I observe.
- I have learned to identify a range of materials, such as wood, plastic and metal.
- I have learned to group materials by how hard or shiny they are.
- I have learned to make and record regular observations of tights stretching, or paper absorbing water.
- I have learned to use a stopwatch.
- I know that windows are made of glass because it is transparent.
- I have learned to explain which paper type absorbed the water fastest.
- I have learned to measure the length of socks and the mass on them when they are stretched.
- I have learned to keep my investigations fair, by only changing one variable at a time.
- I have learned to plot a bar chart of my results.

What do you know?
- Think about these statements.
- Which do you know? Which have you learned?

- I have learned to describe my rocks and how they are different from each other.
- I have learned to say what happens to rocks when I scratch them or put water on them.
- I know and can name a number of common rocks and soils.
- I have learned to group rocks in different ways and explain why I grouped them that way.
- I have learned to describe some ways that new rocks and soils are formed from old.
- I have learned to compare the drainage of water through different soils.
- I have learned to group rock samples by hardness or permeability.
- I have learned to measure the amount of water that drains through soil samples.
- I have learned to explain why different rocks are used for different purposes.
- I have learned to group rocks in different ways with several reasons.
- I have learned to explain hardness and permeability.
- I have learned to record my hardness tests using a table, and my soil permeability tests using a graph, and explain what they show.
- I have learned to link my findings to my knowledge of rocks and soils.

What do you know?

- Think about these statements.
- Which do you know? Which have you learned?

✔

- I have learned to say what I did and what happened.
- I have learned to link what I did to what happened.
- I have learned to describe the changes I made to my spring or magnet.
- I have learned to explain the effect of that change.
- I have learned to link cause and effect: when I added more weights to the spring, it stretched further; when I used a stronger magnet, it attracted over a greater distance.
- I have learned to begin to **generalize**: the more magnets used, the stronger the force; the stronger the spring, the harder it is to stretch.
- I have learned to explain clearly and confidently what I find out about magnets and springs.

Unit 6: Friction checklist

What do you know?

- Think about these statements.
- Which do you know? Which have you learned?

- I have learned to make observations of the way things move.
- I have learned to describe the effects of friction on something I am trying to move.
- I have learned to compare the test results for two or more moving objects.
- I have learned to compare differences in frictional forces – for example, how something moves over different surfaces.
- I have learned to make measurements using a newtonmeter.
- I have learned to explain how different conditions lead to different frictional effects – for example, how rougher surfaces can slow something down.
- I have learned to graph my scientific enquiry results.
- I have learned to explain my scientific enquiry results from what I know about friction.
- I have learned to make a general statement – for example, heavier spinners fall faster, pointed shapes travel faster through water.

Glossary

absorbent – can soak up water

air resistance – a friction force that slows down objects moving through the air

alloy – a mixture of two or more metals

asthma – a medical condition that causes difficulties in breathing

attract – to pull together

bamboo – a tall tropical plant with hollow stems used for making furniture

basalt – a type of dark green-black rock

brittle – splinters or shatters easily

bubble wrap – a sheet of plastic covered with bubbles of air, used for wrapping and protecting things

bungee jumping – a sport in which you jump off something very high with a long length of special, stretchy rope tied to your legs, so that you go up again without touching the ground

butterfly – a way of swimming by lying on your front and moving your arms together over your head, while at the same time moving your legs up and down

canine – a tooth that holds food at the side of the mouth

canopy – the part of the parachute that spreads above you like a roof

carbohydrates – foods that give us rapid energy

carnivore – animals that eat meat

catapult – a small stick in the shape of a Y, with a thin rubber band fastened over the two ends, used to throw stones

ceramic – a hard material, made by firing a non-metallic substance, such as clay, at a very high temperature, making it difficult to break

chisel – metal tool with a sharp edge, used to cut wood or stone

choking – being unable to breathe properly because something is in your throat or there is not enough air

clues – information that helps you understand the reasons why something happens

compare – look for similarities and differences

compost – a mixture of decayed plants, leaves and similar things used to improve the quality of soil

conductor – material that transmits heat, sound or electricity

crunchy – food that is firm or crisp and makes a noise when you bite it

crush – to press something so hard that it breaks or is damaged

decay – to rot away

diet – the kind of foods that people or animals eat – we need a balanced diet to stay healthy

digest – change food that you have just eaten into substances that your body can use

dome – a shape like a ball cut in half

domesticated – animals which are able to work for people or live with them as pets

doughnut shaped – shaped like a ring, with a hole in the middle

drains – flows away

draught – cold air that you can feel moving through a room

dye – a substance you use to change the colour of your clothes, hair, etc.

earthquake – a sudden shaking of the Earth's surface that often causes a lot of damage

elastic – goes back to its original shape after being squashed or stretched

elastic limit – the furthest a material can be stretched and still spring back to its shape

energy – power needed to live, move or work

exercise – moving your body, especially to keep it healthy

experiment – a test to make a discovery, try an idea, or prove something you know

extracted – to take from

fabric – a material made from woven threads

fair test – a science investigation where only one variable is changed and all the others are kept the same

fats – foods that give us a store of energy and help keep us warm

fertile – able to produce good crops or plants

field – area where a force has an effect, e.g. magnetic field around a magnet

fist – the hand when it is tightly closed, so that the fingers are curled towards the palm

flexible – bends easily without breaking

floss – clean your teeth using a thin thread

flower – the part of the plant that makes seeds so the plant can reproduce

force – a push or a pull

forcemeter – spring balance used to measure forces in newtons (N)

friction – a force between touching surfaces

frost – ice that looks white and powdery and covers things that are outside when the temperature is very cold

generalize – form a general principle or opinion based on only a few facts or examples

germinate – when a seed starts to grow into a plant

gooey – sticky and soft

gravel – small stones, used to make a surface for paths, roads, etc.

gravestones – stones above a grave showing details of the person buried there

gravity – the pull of every object towards its centre, especially the Earth

grind – to break something in very small pieces or powder

herbivores – animals that eat only plants

hutch – a small wooden cage that small animals are kept in, especially rabbits

igneous – rocks formed from melted rock inside the Earth

impermeable – doesn't let water through easily

incisor – a tooth that bites and cuts food at the front of the mouth

insulator – material that doesn't transmit heat, sound or electricity

invent – make, design, or create something new

invisible – something that cannot be seen

jewel – a very small stone used in the machinery of a watch

leaf – the part of a plant that uses sunlight to make food

lubricant – something that reduces the friction between surfaces, like oil

magnetic – can be attracted by a magnet

magnifying glass – shaped glass or plastic, used to make objects or print look bigger

man-made – manufactured or artificial; a material that is made by people

manufacturer – a company which makes something for a purpose

marbles – small coloured glass balls that children roll along the ground as part of a game

metal – a strong, shiny material that comes from rocks in the ground

metallic – made of metal or containing metal

metamorphic – rocks changed by temperature or pressure

minerals – simple natural substances needed to help the body stay healthy and develop

molar – a tooth that crushes and grinds food at the back of the mouth

molten – melted by heat

multiply – increase by a large amount

nectar – sweet liquid that bees collect from flowers

newton – unit of force (N)

nutrients – substances needed to grow and be healthy, e.g. vitamins and minerals

nutrition – the act or process of eating and using the nutrients in food for living and growing

odd one out – one that is different from the rest of the group

omnivore – an animal that can eat plants and other animals

oxygen – the gas in the air that plants make and we need to breathe

parachute – something used to slow down a person or object falling through the air

peat – a black substance formed from decaying plants under the surface of the ground

permeable – lets water through easily

plank – a long narrow piece of wooden board, used especially for making structures to walk on

plaque – a white layer that builds up on teeth and can cause them to rot

plastic – a light, strong, man-made material

poles – the ends of a magnet

pollen – a fine dust that makes flowers produce seeds

pop sock – a short stocking that covers the foot and lower part of the leg to the ankle or knee

prediction – what you think will happen in the future

premolar – a tooth that grinds food, positioned between canines and molars

preserve – store food for a long time after treating it so that it will not decay

properties – special qualities of a material

proteins – foods we need to grow

ramp – a slope that has been built to connect two places that are at different levels

reed – a type of tall plant like grass that grows in wet places

repel – to push away

reproduce – to have young

result – outcome of a test

ridge – something long and thin that is higher than the things around it

rigid – doesn't bend easily

rocks – hard natural materials from the Earth

rodent – small animal of the type that has long, sharp front teeth, such as a rat or a rabbit

root – the part of the plant that holds it in the soil and takes up water

rot – decay by a natural process

scent – a pleasant smell that something has

scratch – make a small cut or mark on a surface by pulling something sharp across it

scrunched-up – crushed and twisted into a small round shape

searing – extremely hot

sedimentary – rocks made from layers of rock particles or sediments

seed – a seed grows into a plant, which produces new seeds – seed are how plants reproduce

sieve – a round wire tool with a lot of small holes, used for separating solids from liquids or large objects from smaller ones

slate – a dark-grey rock that can easily be split into flat, thin pieces

snap – break with a sudden, sharp noise

soil – mixture of rock grains and natural materials in which plants grow

spiral – a line in the form of a curve that winds around a central point, moving further away from the centre all the time

spring – a piece of metal wound into a spiral so that it bounces back to its original shape after it is squashed or stretched

squash – press something into a flatter shape

squeeze – to press something firmly together with your fingers and hand

stains – marks that are difficult to remove

stalactite – sharp, pointed object hanging down from the roof of a cave, which is formed gradually by water that contains minerals as it drops slowly from the roof

starches – chemicals made by plants to store sugars

stem – the part of a plant that holds up leaves and flowers

streamlined – specially shaped to reduce resistance when travelling through air or water

sugars – sweet energy foods made by plants

Sun – our main source of light in the daytime – it is our nearest star

surface area – the amount of space covered by something

swell – become larger and rounder than normal

swirls – a twisting circular pattern

synthetic – material that is not natural, but made by people in factories

tap – hit lightly with your fingers

texture – what a surface or material feels like when you touch it

thigh – the top part of your leg, between your knee and your hip

thorn – a sharp point that grows on the stem of a plant

tilted – in a position where one side is higher than the other

tough – resisting breaking, tearing or cutting

transparent – material that lets most light through

treats – special food that tastes good

trough – a low area between two waves of ridges

tug of war – a test of strength in which two teams pull opposite ends of a rope against each other

uncoiled – stretched out

vampire bat – a South American bat that sucks the blood of other animals

vegetables – edible plants or parts of plants

vitamins – chemicals needed by the body for healthy growth

volcanic eruption – when a volcano (mountain with a large hole at the top through which lava is forced out) explodes

waterlogged – something flooded with water, which cannot be used

waterproof – a material that stops water passing through

water resistance – a friction force that slows down objects moving through water

wax – solid substance made of fat or oil and used to make candles, polish, etc.

zigzag – a pattern that looks like a line of 'z's joined together

Index